Step-by-Step Classic Kitchen

Desserts

A hundred graded recipes with kitchen hints and wine guide

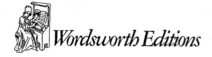
Wordsworth Editions

CHARLOTTE
AUX FRUITS ROUGES
PAGE 42

Step-by-Step Classic Kitchen

Eggs, butter, cream, sugar – the basic ingredients of nearly all the recipes included in this book, but the range and variety of taste and texture achieved with them is truly amazing. Smooth mousses and charlottes, melting soufflés, crisp and appetizing pancakes and fritters . . . all enhanced (many, of course, by the subtle addition of wine or liqueur) with any number of different flavourings – the traditional rum with chocolate, or walnut with coffee, but have you thought of apples baked with redcurrant jelly and cinnamon, or a sweet soufflé of spiced pumpkin?

The classic French desserts are naturally included – crêpes Suzette, caramel cream, oeufs à la neige, as well as basic recipes for egg custard, crème pâtissière, a quick pancake batter. Perhaps most surprising to the English cook is the new slant given to desserts and puddings remembered without enthusiasm from childhood days – a remarkable blancmange, for example, made with cream and almonds, the flavours all subtly blended, in every way utterly unlike that tasteless lump of wallpaper paste that used to quiver on our plates. And rice and bread puddings, too, come into their own when flavoured with honey and cinnamon, or studded with fresh cherries that have been soaked in kirsch.

To the French cook, appearance and presentation of a dish is every bit as important as its taste and flavour, and here there are many exciting suggestions with a strong visual emphasis: a snow-white cream dessert served with a bright red sauce of puréed fruit, for instance. The charlottes and gâteaux are stunningly presented, as you might expect, with piped cream decorations and ingenious and imaginative garnishes. And – particularly with children in mind perhaps – many of the desserts have been amusingly designed round a pictorial theme – a coconut igloo with icing sugar snow; pear hedgehogs with almonds for prickles and currants for eyes.

Don't be put off by the thought of new and complicated methods of preparation. The clear step-by-step instructions will guide you successfully through every recipe. Experiment with these exciting new ideas and you will have a range of desserts at your fingertips that will add a whole new dimension to your cooking for family and guests. For no meal, not even the simplest, is complete without a dessert . . .

Table of Contents

Each dish is followed by its total preparation and cooking time. (See note 1 on facing page.)

The star (★) system used throughout the book, indicating the degree of simplicity or difficulty of each recipe, is as follows:

★ *Very easy*   ★★ *Easy*   ★ ★ ★ *Difficult*

Pancakes

Fritters

Fruit Desserts

Notes: Getting the Best out of this Book

1. The preparation times given in the Table of Contents and with each recipe are minimum times: they will vary according to the cook's ability and the equipment available. Certain of the recipes require periods for macerating or chilling. These have not been taken into account in the times given in the table, but are indicated in the recipes.
2. It is best to use double cream for most recipes – it is the nearest equivalent to French cream. Remember also that the French use unsalted butter, and this is assumed in the recipes unless otherwise stated.
3. Certain of the recipes require cooking *au bain-marie*. This consists of placing whatever is to be cooked in a saucepan inside a larger saucepan filled with almost-boiling water. This method is ideal for cooking certain delicate sauces or other dishes which would react badly if exposed to a direct heat.
4. Oven temperatures. The following are Gas, Fahrenheit and Centigrade equivalents:

Gas	¼	½	1	2	3	4	5	6	7	8	9
°F	225	250	275	300	325	350	375	400	425	450	475
°C	110	120	140	160	170	180	190	200	220	230	250

5. It is important when using these recipes to follow the exact proportions. A set of kitchen scales, measuring jug, glass and spoons are essential. Follow either metric *or* avoirdupois measurements in each recipe.
6. To help you choose the right wine for your meal, see page 80.

Crème Panachée Chocolat-Orange
Chocolate and Orange Cream Dessert

Serves 2. Preparation and cooking: 30 min
2 hr before serving ★

○ **400ml (14 fl oz) orange juice**
○ **200ml (7 fl oz) milk**
○ **15ml (1 tbls) unsweetened cocoa**
○ **60ml (4 tbls) cornflour**
○ **90ml (6 tbls) sugar**

1. Prepare the orange cream: put 60ml (4 tbls) of sugar together with 45ml (3 tbls) of cornflour in a medium-sized saucepan; mix well and gradually pour in the orange juice, stirring all the time. Place the saucepan over a medium heat and bring to the boil; boil for 1 minute, stirring continuously; then remove from the heat.
2. Prepare the chocolate cream: put the cocoa, 30ml (2 tbls) of sugar and 15ml (1 tbls) of cornflour in a small saucepan. Mix well, then gradually add the cold milk, stirring all the time. Place over a medium heat and bring to the boil. Boil for 1 minute, stirring continuously, and remove from the heat.
3. Pour into two tall, straight glasses in the following manner: first pour the orange cream into the bottom of each glass, which should be held at a slight angle. Leave the glasses in the freezer for 5 minutes, keeping them tilted; then remove, and pour half the chocolate cream into each glass, still at an inclined angle. Put them back in the freezer for 5 minutes. Now set the glasses upright and pour in the rest of the orange cream. Place in the refrigerator for at least 2 hours before serving.

Just before serving, decorate with maraschino cherries. You can make the same dessert with different flavoured creams, such as pineapple, bilberry, tangerine or lemon.

Crème Soufflée aux Quatre Parfums
Cream Soufflé with Four Flavourings

Serves 6. Preparation and cooking: 20 min
2 hr before serving ★★

○ **¾ litre (27 fl oz) milk**
○ **15ml (1 tbls) good quality instant coffee**
○ **30ml (2 tbls) crystallized caramel**
○ **45ml (3 tbls) unsweetened cocoa**
○ **2.5ml (½ tsp) powdered vanilla**
○ **5 eggs**
○ **120g (4¾ oz) caster sugar**

1. Put the coffee, cocoa, caramel and vanilla in a saucepan. Mix all the ingredients together and pour the milk in gradually, stirring all the time. Place over a low heat, but do not allow to boil.
2. Break one of the eggs into another saucepan. Separate the other four eggs, putting the whites in a large bowl and adding the yolks to the saucepan. Sprinkle in the sugar and beat well into the egg yolks until the mixture becomes lighter in colour. Then pour in the flavoured milk, stirring continuously.
3. Place the saucepan over a low heat and cook without boiling, stirring all the time. Remove from the heat when the custard has thickened so that it coats the back of a spoon.
4. Strain the custard through a fine sieve. Beat the egg whites until stiff and fold into the warm custard, beating well until the mixture is smooth and light.
5. Leave to cool and place in the refrigerator for at least 1 hour before serving.

Serve with biscuits such as sponge fingers or with slices of sponge cake. This dessert does not keep well, and should be eaten the same day.

Crème Pâtissière Veloutée

Serves 6. Preparation and cooking: 30 min
1 hr before serving
★

Rich Crème Pâtissière

○ **½ litre (18 fl oz) milk**
○ **4 egg yolks**
○ **40g (1¾ oz) cornflour**
○ **150g (6 oz) caster sugar**
○ **½ litre (18 fl oz) double cream**
  or whipping cream
○ **1 vanilla pod**

To flavour:
○ **30ml (2 tbls) kirsch, or rum, or**
  grand marnier

1. Blend the cornflour with 60ml (4 tbls) of milk in a bowl. Split the vanilla pod lengthways and put in a saucepan with the rest of the milk. Bring to the boil, turn off heat and leave to infuse for 5 minutes.
2. Meanwhile, beat the egg yolks with the sugar in another saucepan, until the mixture becomes lighter in colour. Then add the blended cornflour and milk and stir well for 30 seconds. Remove the vanilla pod from the warm milk, and pour in to the pan gradually. Mix well and place over a medium heat: allow to boil for 2 minutes, stirring all the time. Place the pan in a basin of cold water and leave to cool, stirring frequently to make sure that a skin does not form on the surface. If you wish, you can brush the surface with a knob of butter or cover it with a sheet of greaseproof paper, so that you will not have to stir it.
3. When the crème pâtissière is cold, add the flavouring you want. Beat the cream until stiff and fold into the crème pâtissière, lifting from the bottom up towards the top with a spatula.
4. Pour the crème pâtissière into individual bowls and leave to refrigerate for at least one hour before serving.

You may add more or less whipped cream according to taste. Without the addition of the whipped cream this crème pâtissière is used as a filling for cakes and pastries. Like this, it is a dessert in its own right. Serve with various kinds of biscuits.

Crème Chantilly can be made quickly and easily, in only 10 minutes. For 1 litre (1¾ pints) you will need 500g (18 oz) of chilled double cream (or whipping cream), a small amount of vanilla sugar and 15ml (1 tbls) of caster sugar. If you like you can substitute 100ml (3½ fl oz) of cold milk for some of the cream.

Make sure that the bowl you use has been chilled first; the cream and milk must be very cold indeed if this recipe is going to work successfully. Keep them in the coldest part of the refrigerator for an hour or so before you start to make it. You can place the bowl in a larger bowl of ice cubes while you are doing the beating.

Pour the cream or the cream and milk into the chilled bowl and beat it slowly (using an electric beater or a wire whisk) until it becomes foamy, lifting the cream as you whip it. Gradually increase the speed and continue until the cream is stiff and stands up into peaks. Then beat in the vanilla sugar and the caster sugar. The amount of sugar you use can vary according to what you are going to do with the cream, and the sweetness of the other ingredients of the dessert.

When the cream is very stiff, stop beating. If you beat it for too long it may become granular and begin to turn into butter, but if the cream is chilled first, this is less likely to happen.

Crème Anglaise

Egg Custard

Serves 6. Preparation and cooking: 20 min

★ ★

○ **1 litre (1¾ pints) milk**
○ **8 egg yolks**
○ **150g (6 oz) caster sugar**
○ **1 vanilla pod**

1. With a sharp knife, split the vanilla pod lengthways. Put in a saucepan with the milk and bring to the boil; then turn the heat off and leave to infuse for 5 minutes.
2. Meanwhile, put the egg yolks in a heavy bottomed enamelled or stainless steel saucepan (aluminium will taint the cream and give it an unpleasant taste). Sprinkle in the sugar slowly, folding it into the egg yolks with a wooden spoon or spatula. If you pour all the sugar in at once over the egg yolks, it will literally 'cook' them and make them hard. Beat the mixture well with a spatula or whisk until it becomes lighter in colour, thick and frothy, and has doubled in volume. Then pour in the warm milk, drop by drop at first so that it blends perfectly with the egg mixture, then more rapidly.
3. Place the saucepan over a low heat – the mixture must not boil. Stir continuously with a wooden spoon or spatula in a circular movement, making sure that your spoon reaches right round the bottom and sides of the pan. In 5 to 10 minutes the mixture will have thickened. While it is cooking the froth on the surface will disappear, starting at the centre and moving outwards to the edge of the pan, as the custard gradually thickens. When the froth has completely vanished, the custard is ready: it should coat the spoon smoothly and evenly, and if you draw a line across it, it should stay there. Now remove the saucepan from the heat and quickly strain the custard through a fine sieve into a cold basin, which should preferably be standing in a larger one filled with cold water. It must be done quickly so that the custard stops cooking; otherwise the eggs will curdle. If this happens, do not despair: place the saucepan in cold water to stop any further cooking and beat the custard vigorously with a whisk or electric beater. It should soon become light, smooth and creamy. Leave to cool, stirring from time to time to make sure that a 'skin' does not appear on the surface.

You may need a little experience before you can be sure this egg custard will succeed every time; the first time you try it, you can add 5ml (1 tsp) of cornflour to the cold milk to make sure the custard does not curdle.

This custard makes a perfect sauce to serve with all kinds of biscuits and *brioches*, cream-filled cakes, charlottes, bavaroises, hot puddings, 'floating islands', and with stewed and puréed fruit.

The quantities given are variable. For a lighter custard, use only 6 egg yolks; or you may add as many as 12 egg yolks if you want it really rich and creamy. For extra richness, you may add 200ml (7 fl oz) of whipped cream or crème Chantilly once the custard has cooled.

For coffee custard, add 15ml (1 tbls) of instant coffee, or 30-45ml (2-3 tbls) of freshly ground coffee to the milk, and leave to infuse for a few minutes before pouring on to the egg yolks. Even better, flavour with chocolate by adding 30ml (2 tbls) of unsweetened cocoa to the milk, or 50 to 80g (2-3 oz) of plain bitter chocolate. More or less sugar may be added according to taste, whether the custard is flavoured, or what dessert it is to be served with.

Crème Suave à la Mandarine
Tangerine Cream Dessert

Serves 8. Preparation and cooking: 30 min
2 hr before serving
★ ★

○ **6 tangerines**
○ **½ litre (18 fl oz) milk**
○ **½ litre (18 fl oz) double cream**
○ **2 eggs**
○ **6 egg yolks**
○ **100g (4 oz) caster sugar**
○ **100g (4 oz) sugar lumps**
○ **100ml (3½ fl oz) tangerine liqueur**
○ **200g (7 oz) sponge cake or fingers, or macaroons**

1. Wipe the outsides of the tangerines and rub the sugar lumps over them.
2. Bring the milk to the boil, then leave to cool. When lukewarm, add the flavoured sugar lumps and let them dissolve.
3. Break the 2 eggs into a saucepan, and add the 6 egg yolks; sprinkle in the sugar and beat until the mixture has turned pale and frothy. Pour in the lukewarm milk, beating continuously; then beat in the cream. Place the saucepan over a low heat and cook until the custard thickens just enough to coat a spoon or spatula smoothly – but do not let it boil! Remove from the heat and strain through a fine sieve into a bowl. To cool the custard quickly, place the bowl in a larger dish filled with cold water.
4. While the custard is cooling, squeeze the tangerines, and strain the juice through a fine sieve into a bowl. Add 30ml (2 tbls) of the tangerine liqueur. Stir well.
5. When it is cold, add the rest of the tangerine liqueur to the cream, stirring well, and pour one-third of the mixture into a glass serving dish or bowl. Soak the sponge cake or fingers, or the macaroons, in the tangerine juice and liqueur and lay half of them on top of the cream. Pour in another third of the tangerine cream and place the rest of the biscuits on top. Slowly pour the remaining third of the cream over to finish, and refrigerate for at least 2 hours before serving.

If you decide to serve this dessert in individual glasses, first place a piece of sponge finger or macaroon at the bottom of each before pouring in the tangerine cream.

Crème Soufflée au Café
Coffee Cream Soufflé

Serves 4-5. Preparation and cooking: 15 min
1 hr before serving
★

○ **4 eggs**
○ **100g (4 oz) sugar**
○ **15ml (1 tbls) instant coffee**
○ **250ml (9 fl oz) milk**
○ **200ml (7 fl oz) double cream**

1. Bring the milk to the boil. Separate the eggs putting the whites in a large basin and the yolks in a saucepan. Sprinkle the sugar over the yolks and beat in until the mixture has turned pale and frothy.
2. Beat the egg whites until stiff. When the milk starts to boil, turn the heat off and sprinkle in the coffee; stir well and pour the milk a little at a time into the egg yolks and sugar. Then beat in the cream. Place the saucepan over a low heat and cook, stirring continuously, until it coats the back of a spoon smoothly. Remove from the heat and add the beaten egg whites all at once. Fold in quickly with a spatula and pour the soufflé into a bowl. Leave to cool.
3. When cool, you may leave the soufflé in the refrigerator for one hour, but do not serve it too cold.

Serve with *petits-fours*. You may add 50g (2 oz) of freshly ground coffee to the milk, and leave to infuse, to give this dessert a more delicate flavour.

The bark of the cinnamon tree is most easily bought as a finely ground powder. You can also find thin pieces of the peeled bark that have been dried to form curled-up 'quills'; or you can buy it as sticks. The essence of the spice can be extracted as a transparent liquid; in this form its flavour is extremely concentrated, and it must be used very sparingly.

Petits Pots de Crème au Café

Coffee Ramekins

Serves 6. Preparation: 10 min Cooking: 40 min
4 hr before serving
★

○ **200ml (7 fl oz) very strong warm coffee**
○ **600ml (22 fl oz) cream (preferably double cream)**
○ **100g (4 oz) caster sugar**
○ **8 egg yolks**

1. Preheat the oven to 195°C (375°F; gas mark 5). Heat the cream but do not let it boil. Put the egg yolks into a bowl and sprinkle in the sugar. Beat the mixture until it has turned pale and frothy. Then pour in the warm coffee, bit by bit, and the cream, beating in well with a spatula or whisk.
2. Pour the cream mixture into 6 individual ramekins, straining it through a fine sieve.
3. Place the ramekins in a *bain-marie* or large ovenproof dish filled with water, and cook in the oven for 40 minutes. Check whether they are cooked by inserting the blade of a knife into the centre of one of the ramekins. It should come out quite dry and clean. Make sure the water in the *bain-marie* does not boil.
4. When ready, remove the ramekins from the oven and leave to cool. Refrigerate for at least 4 hours before serving.

Crème Brûlée

Crème Brûlée (with caramel topping)

Serves 6-7. Preparation and cooking: 1 hr
the day before serving
★

○ **1 litre (1¾ pints) double cream**
○ **2 eggs**
○ **10 egg yolks**
○ **100g (4 oz) caster sugar**
○ **5ml (1 tsp) vanilla essence**

For the caramel:
○ **60ml (4 tbls) caster sugar**

1. You must make this dessert the day before. Set the oven to 180°C (350°F; gas mark 4). Break 2 eggs into a bowl, and add the 10 egg yolks, then the vanilla and 30ml (2 tbls) of cream. Put the rest of the cream in a saucepan over a low heat, and heat until it 'shivers', but do not let it boil.
2. Meanwhile, sprinkle the sugar on to the eggs in the bowl, beating well until the mixture turns pale and frothy.
3. Pour the warm cream over the egg and sugar mixture, a little at a time, beating continuously. Then strain through a fine sieve into an ovenproof dish 24cm (9½ inches) in diameter.
4. Place the dish in a *bain-marie* and cook in the oven for approximately 45 minutes, or until the blade of a knife comes out clean. Make sure the water in the *bain-marie* does not boil, otherwise the eggs in the mixture may curdle.
5. When it is cooked, remove from the oven and leave to cool. Leave at the top of the refrigerator overnight.
6. The next day, 10 minutes before serving, heat the grill; place some ice cubes in the grill pan. Sprinkle some sugar over the cream and place under the grill. When the sugar has caramelized (after 3 or 4 minutes), remove from the grill and bring to the table.

It is easier to caramelize the cream when it is very cold. You may then replace it in the refrigerator and serve it very well chilled. You should then be able to crack the caramel topping with a spoon, like a pane of glass.

If you are cooking a cream dessert in individual ramekins or pots in a bain-marie *over a low heat, place them on a wire rack in a large saucepan or flameproof casserole filled with water and cook covered.*

Crème Renversée aux Poires

Serves 5. Preparation: 15 min Cooking: 55 min

★

Cream Mould with Pears

○ **500g (1 lb 2 oz) William or Comice pears**
○ **250ml (9 fl oz) milk**
○ **250ml (9 fl oz) single cream**
○ **200g (7 oz) caster sugar**
○ **1 vanilla pod**
○ **3 eggs**
○ **1 egg yolk**

1. Set the oven to 190°C (365°F; gas mark 4½). Split the vanilla pod in two lengthways. Place with the milk in a saucepan and bring to the boil. Turn the heat off, cover, and leave to infuse.
2. In a small saucepan, put 60ml (4 tbls) of sugar (about 80g/3¼ oz); add 30ml (2 tbls) of water, and stir over a medium heat. When the sugar has turned golden, pour into a mould or sandwich tin 22cm (8½ inches) in diameter. Tilt the mould in all directions so that the bottom and halfway up the sides is filmed with the caramel.
3. Quarter the pears, peel and remove the core; slice thinly and roughly layer the pieces in the mould.
4. Put the rest of the sugar in a bowl. Add the 2 eggs and the yolk of another. Beat well until the mixture is smooth; then add the warm milk (take out the vanilla pod first), beating all the time. Finally add the cream. Pour the mixture over the pears in the mould and cook in the oven for 55 minutes. Do not let the custard boil. When cooked, it should be springy to the finger, and the blade of a knife should come out clean. Leave to cool before turning it out on to a serving dish.

Crème Renversée au Vin Cuit

Serves 6. Preparation: 25 min Cooking: 45 min
2 hr before serving
★

Cream Mould with Spiced Wine

○ **1 bottle of white wine: sauternes, monbazillac, anjou, etc**
○ **6 eggs**
○ **2 egg yolks**
○ **200g (7 oz) caster sugar**
○ **1 5cm (2 inch) stick of cinnamon**
○ **2 cloves**
○ **4 coriander seeds**

1. Put the sugar, coriander, cloves and cinnamon in a saucepan with the wine. Bring to the boil, over a medium heat, stirring with a spatula; then reduce the heat and let it 'shiver' for 15 minutes in the uncovered saucepan. Turn the heat off and leave to cool for 5 minutes.
2. Set the oven to 195°C (375°F; gas mark 5). Beat the 6 eggs and 2 egg yolks together in a bowl until the mixture starts to froth. Then add 30ml (2 tbls) of the warm wine, mix together well and pour into the rest of the wine, beating vigorously.
3. Strain through a fine sieve into a mould or sandwich tin 22cm (8½ inches) in diameter. Place in a *bain-marie* and cook in the oven for 45 minutes or more, until the blade of a knife inserted in the centre comes out clean. Make sure the water in the *bain-marie* does not boil.
4. When it is cooked, remove from the oven and leave to cool. You may serve it at room temperature, or you may refrigerate it before turning it out on to a serving dish.

The sugar may be replaced with a scented honey; you may line the mould with caramel. If you cook the dessert in individual pots you will not need to unmould it, and so you only need use 3 egg whites. Serve with a fresh fruit salad or with a *coulis* of red soft fruits. For this you will need 400ml (14 fl oz) of puréed fruit (raspberries, strawberries, redcurrants), 100g (4 oz) of sugar, the juice of one lemon and one orange. Mix together and chill. It is deliciously refreshing!

Crème Renversée au Caramel

Caramel Cream

Serves 8. Preparation: 15 min Cooking: 45 min-1 hr at least 6 hr before serving ★

○ **1 litre (1¾ pints) milk**
○ **8 eggs**
○ **100g (4 oz) sugar**
○ **1 vanilla pod**

For the caramel:
○ **100g (4 oz) sugar**
○ **5ml (1 tsp) lemon juice**

1. Set the oven to 195°C (375°F; gas mark 5). Split the vanilla pod in two lengthways. Put the vanilla and milk into a saucepan and bring to the boil. Then turn the heat off, and leave to infuse.

2. Prepare the caramel: put the sugar in a small saucepan together with 30ml (2 tbls) of water and the lemon juice. Place over a medium heat and when the sugar has turned golden, turn the heat off. Pour the caramel into a fluted mould (2 litres/3½ pints capacity) or charlotte mould, or you can use a soufflé mould. Tilt the mould in your hands so that the bottom and sides are filmed with the caramel.

3. Break the eggs in a bowl; add the sugar and beat with a whisk until the mixture is smooth; then pour in the milk, having removed the vanilla pod. Continue beating and pour the mixture into the caramelized mould, straining it through a fine sieve. Place the mould in a *bain-marie* and cook in the oven for 45 minutes, until the blade of a knife inserted in the centre comes out clean.

4. Remove the mould from the oven and leave to cool for at least 4 hours before unmoulding. To unmould, place a deep serving dish upside down over the mould and quickly turn the two over. You may leave the caramel cream in the refrigerator for a few hours. It will then be easier to unmould if you first place it in a tin filled with warm water for 30 seconds.

You may serve this caramel cream as it is, or you may pour some liquid caramel over it. To prepare the caramel, use 150g (6 oz) of sugar mixed with 100ml (3½ fl oz) of water. This recipe is simple and economical. If you want the caramel cream to be less springy and smoother, use fewer egg whites and replace them with egg yolks; but remember that you will always need 4 egg whites to ensure that the dessert is firm and unmoulds easily.

This cream caramel may also be served in ramekins or individual dishes. You may also add a piece of orange or lemon peel to the milk with the vanilla; it will give more flavour! Or you can make a chocolate or coffee flavoured custard instead of the caramel by adding 50g (2 oz) of unsweetened cocoa or 30ml (2 tbls) of instant coffee to the milk; you will also need an extra 50g (2 oz) of sugar. The caramel used to line the mould may replace the 100g (4 oz) of sugar given in the above recipe. All you need do is add the caramel while it is still liquid to the boiling milk; blend together well, then pour (it should be warm and not boiling) over the beaten eggs. Grease the mould before pouring in the custard.

Mousses, custards and creams need to be cooked in a bain-marie *(that is, in a tin half-filled with water) in the oven or placed over the heat. This is to prevent the eggs in the mixture from cooking too fast and curdling.*

Make sure that the water in the bain-marie *is 'shivering' and never begins to boil; if it does, add a little cold water to reduce the heat. If the water evaporates so that the* bain-marie *is less than half-full, add more warm water.*

When using a bain-marie *in the oven, place the mould or ramekins in a large baking tin or ovenproof dish filled with water. When cooking over the heat, put the custard or cream in a small saucepan and place it inside a larger one half-filled with water.*

Crème Renversée au Caramel ▶

Petits Pots de Crème au Chocolat

Chocolate Ramekins

Serves 8. Preparation: 15 min
Cooking: 40 min 3 hr before serving
★

○ **1 litre (1¾ pints) milk**
○ **150g (6 oz) plain bitter chocolate**
○ **60ml (4 tbls) unsweetened cocoa**
○ **1 vanilla pod**
○ **1 egg**
○ **6 egg yolks**
○ **150g (6 oz) caster sugar**

1. Set the oven at 195°C (375°F; gas mark 5). Split the vanilla pod in two lengthways. Place the cocoa and sugar in a saucepan and pour in the milk, a little at a time, stirring well to dissolve the cocoa and sugar; then add the vanilla, and break in the chocolate.
2. Cook over a low heat, stirring with a spoon or spatula until the chocolate melts, making sure it does not boil. Then turn the heat off and leave to cool for 5 minutes.
3. Beat the egg and 6 egg yolks together in a bowl and blend with 30ml (2 tbls) of the chocolate flavoured milk. Beat well once more, then add to the rest of the milk in the saucepan, beating continuously.
4. Fill 8 ovenproof ramekins with the custard, straining it through a fine sieve. Place the ramekins in a *bain-marie* and cook in the oven for 40 minutes. They are ready when the blade of a knife inserted in the centre of one of the ramekins comes out clean.
5. Remove the ramekins from the oven and leave to cool. Then refrigerate for at least 2 hours before serving.

Petits Pots de Crème au Porto

Ramekins of Cream with Port

Serves 6. Preparation: 15 min Cooking: 40 min
4 hr before serving
★

○ **½ litre (18 fl oz) milk**
○ **300ml (10½ fl oz) single cream**
○ **150g (6 oz) caster sugar**
○ **6 egg yolks**
○ **30ml (2 tbls) port**

1. Set the oven at 195°C (375°F; gas mark 5). Put the sugar in a saucepan with 45ml (3 tbls) of water and cook over a medium heat until it has formed a light caramel.
2. Heat the milk and the cream together. When the caramel is ready, remove the saucepan from the heat and pour the warm milk/cream mixture over. Stir continuously until the caramel has completely dissolved.
3. Put the egg yolks and port in a bowl, and beat with a whisk until the mixture starts to froth. Then pour in the caramelized milk, a little at a time, beating continuously.
4. Fill 6 ramekins with the custard, straining it through a fine sieve. Place in a *bain-marie* and cook in the oven for 40 minutes. Check by inserting the blade of a knife to see if they are ready.
5. Remove the ramekins from the oven and leave to cook. Refrigerate for at least 4 hours before serving.

Flan

Baked Custard

★

○ **½ litre (18 fl oz) milk**
○ **6 eggs**
○ **150g (6 oz) caster sugar**
○ **1 vanilla pod**
○ **1 lemon**
○ **100g (4 oz) flour**
○ **20g (¾ oz) butter**

1. Set the oven at 220°C (425°F; gas mark 7). Split the vanilla pod in two lengthways. Peel the lemon with a sharp knife, leaving the pith. Put the vanilla and spiral of lemon peel in a small saucepan with the milk and bring to the boil. Turn the heat off and leave for about 5 minutes.
2. Meanwhile, grease a mould or sandwich tin 24cm (9½ inches) in diameter. Break the eggs into a bowl, sprinkle in the sugar, and beat until the mixture turns pale and frothy. Then sprinkle in the sifted flour. Continue beating until the mixture is smooth and well blended. Remove the vanilla pod and lemon peel and pour the milk into the bowl, a little at a time, beating continuously. Beat for another 2 minutes so that the flour is completely incorporated in the milk and will not sink to the bottom during cooking.
3. Strain the custard through a fine sieve into the mould, and cook in the oven for 40 minutes. Insert the blade of a knife into the centre to see if it is cooked.
4. Remove the mould from the oven and leave to cool. Serve in the mould, or turn out on to a serving dish.

This simple recipe is always a success with young and old alike. You may replace the lemon peel with some orange flower water for variation.

Flan de Potiron aux Épices

Baked Custard with Spiced Pumpkin

★

○ **1kg (2¼ lb) slice of pumpkin**
○ **⅓ litre (10½ fl oz) milk**
○ **100g (4 oz) caster sugar**
○ **3 eggs**
○ **3 pinches powdered ginger**
○ **3 pinches grated nutmeg**
○ **1.5ml (¼ tsp) powdered cinnamon**
○ **3 pinches ground pepper**
○ **3 pinches salt**
○ **30ml (2 tbls) flour**
○ **20g (¾ oz) butter**

1. Peel and cut the pumpkin into large cubes. Place in a saucepan with the milk and salt and simmer over a low heat for approximately 15 minutes, until the pumpkin is tender; then pass through a vegetable mill or blender.
2. Set the oven at 200°C (387°F; gas mark 5½). Break the eggs in a bowl, sprinkle in the sugar and flour, and beat well for 1 minute. Add the pumpkin purée, ginger, nutmeg, cinnamon and pepper. Mix all together well.
3. Grease a mould or sandwich tin 22cm (8½ inches) in diameter. Pour in the custard and place in a *bain-marie*. Cook in the oven for between 45 minutes and 1 hour, until the custard is firm.
4. Remove from the oven and leave to cool completely, then place in the refrigerator for at least 4 hours before serving. Turn out on to a dish and serve.

To shorten the cooking time, you may pour the custard into individual ramekins. Try adding 30ml (2 tbls) of currants or 6 chopped prunes, or even some slices of apple, to the custard before cooking. For even greater flavour, add the finely grated peel of one lemon or half an orange.

Flan de Chocolat à l'Orange

Serves 6-8. Preparation: 20 min Cooking: 45 min

Baked Chocolate Custard with Orange

★★

○ **125g (5 oz) fondant chocolate**
○ **100g (4 oz) caster sugar**
○ **65g (2¾ oz) butter**
○ **6 eggs**
○ **1 orange**
○ **15ml (1 tbls) flour**

For the icing:
○ **75g (3 oz) fondant chocolate**
○ **60g (2½ oz) butter**
○ **30ml (2 tbls) orange liqueur**

1. Separate the eggs; place the whites in a large bowl and reserve the yolks. Put the grated peel of the orange in a medium-sized saucepan, then add the squeezed juice. Add the sugar (reserving 30ml (2 tbls)) and cook over a very low heat, stirring with a spoon or spatula until the sugar has melted. Then break in the chocolate and cook until it melts, placing an asbestos sheet in between the saucepan and the heat.
2. Grease a mould or sandwich tin 24cm (9½ inches) in diameter with a little of the butter. Remove the saucepan with the chocolate mixture from the heat and add the rest of the butter, mixing well. Add the egg yolks, one by one, beating briskly; then sprinkle in the flour. Beat well.
3. Set the oven at 187°C (362°F; gas mark 4½). Beat the egg whites lightly and add the remaining 30ml (2 tbls) of sugar. Beat for another 10 seconds before folding quickly in to the custard, a third at a time, lifting the spoon from the bottom to the top. Pour in to the mould and cook in the oven for 45 minutes. Remove from the oven and leave to cool for 5 minutes. Turn out on to a serving dish.
4. Make an icing for the baked custard when it is cold. Break the chocolate into a small basin, add 15ml (1 tbls) of water and place over a saucepan of simmering water until it melts (make sure the water does not boil). Add the butter and orange liqueur, remove from the heat and blend together well, using a spatula. Pour this mixture over the custard and spread evenly with a palette knife.

Flan à l'Ananas

Serves 6-8. Preparation: 30 min Cooking: 1 hr 15 min
6 hr before serving

Baked Pineapple Custard

★★★

○ **1 pineapple, weighing about 1.2kg (2¾ lb)**
○ **300g (11 oz) caster sugar**
○ **6 eggs**
○ **50g (2 oz) flour**
○ **5ml (1 tsp) vanilla essence**
○ **30ml (2 tbls) white rum**
○ **juice of 1 lime**

1. Peel and dice the pineapple, making sure you cut out the woody core. Pass through a vegetable mill or blender; then through a sieve. Put this juice in to a saucepan with 200g (7 oz) of the sugar. Place over a low heat and bring to a gentle boil for 2 minutes. Remove from the heat.
2. Set the oven at 195°C (375°F; gas mark 5). Put the rest of the sugar in a small saucepan with 30ml (2 tbls) of water and cook gently until you have a golden syrup. Pour this into a mould or sandwich tin 22cm (8½ inches) in diameter, tilting it so that the syrup coats the bottom and sides evenly.
3. Break the eggs in a bowl, sprinkle in the flour, and beat well until the mixture starts to froth. Then add 30ml (2 tbls) of the pineapple juice and beat well; beat in the remaining juice.
4. Add the lime juice, vanilla essence and rum. Mix in well and pour into the mould. Cook in a *bain-marie* in the oven for 1 hour and 15 minutes until the surface of the custard is firm.
5. When it is cooked, leave to cool completely, and refrigerate for at least 6 hours before serving. If you first place the mould in hot water for 20 seconds, you will be able to unmould it easily, turning it out on to a serving dish.

Crème Pâtissière Veloutée (p8) ▶

Flan de Pommes Caramélisé aux Noix

Baked Caramel Custard with Apples and Walnuts

Serves 6. Preparation: 50 min
Cooking: 45 min
★ ★

○ **1.5kg (3¼ lb) apples**
○ **180g (7¼ oz) caster sugar**
○ **4 eggs**
○ **1 lemon**
○ **30ml (2 tbls) double cream**
○ **8 walnuts**

1. Preheat the oven to 220°C (425°F; gas mark 7). Quarter the apples, peel and remove the core. Slice them thinly and place in an ovenproof casserole. Cook covered in the oven for 30 minutes.
2. Shell the walnuts and grate them coarsely. Grate the lemon and squeeze the juice.
3. Put 120g (4¾ oz) of the sugar in a saucepan with 30ml (2 tbls) of water and 5ml (1 tsp) of lemon juice. Do not add the lemon peel. Cook over a medium heat until you have a golden syrup. Turn the heat off and add 15ml (1 tbls) of water. Stir in well, then pour the caramel in to a mould or sandwich tin 22cm (8½ inches) in diameter, tilting it so that the caramel coats the bottom and sides evenly. Sprinkle in the coarsely grated walnuts.
4. After the apples have cooked for 30 minutes, remove from the oven and reduce the heat to 195°C (375°F; gas mark 5). Pass the apples through a vegetable mill or blender and put the purée in a saucepan with the remaining sugar and the cream. Cook over a medium heat, stirring with a spatula, until the purée thickens and turns slightly golden.
5. Turn the heat off and add the rest of the lemon juice to the purée with the lemon peel. Stir well and break the eggs in one by one, folding them in with a spatula. Pour the mixture into the mould, smoothing the surface flat with a spatula. Cook in a *bain-marie* in the oven for 45 minutes.
6. After that time, check whether the custard is ready by pressing the centre lightly with your fingertips: if it is firm and springy, it is cooked. Otherwise, leave in the oven for a little longer. Then remove the dish from the oven and leave to cool for 20 minutes; turn out on to a serving dish. This dessert may be eaten slightly warm, cold, or chilled.

Flan aux Fruits Râpés

Baked Fruit Custard

Serves 6-7. Preparation: 15 min Cooking: 1 hr
★

○ **⅓ litre (7½ fl oz) milk**
○ **100g (4 oz) single cream**
○ **3 eggs**
○ **45ml (3 tbls) flour**
○ **90ml (6 tbls) caster sugar**
○ **5ml (1 tsp) powdered vanilla**
○ **1 large apple**
○ **1 large pear**
○ **1 large banana**
○ **30ml (2 tbls) currants**
○ **15ml (1 tbls) rum**
○ **1 lemon**
○ **25g (1 oz) butter**

1. Set the oven at 205°C (400°F; gas mark 6). Leave the currants to soak in the rum. Mix the sugar with the vanilla. Break the eggs in to a bowl; stir in the mixed sugar and vanilla, reserving 15ml (1 tbls), and sprinkle in the flour. Stir well until the mixture is smooth and well-blended. Then add the milk and cream, mixing in well.
2. Grease an ovenproof dish or a mould or sandwich tin 24cm (9½ inches) in diameter. Peel the apple, remove the core, and grate it coarsely into the custard. Mix well. Grate the pear and banana in the same way and mix everything together well.
3. Now finely grate the lemon peel over the bowl. Add the currants soaked in rum and mix once more. Pour the mixture into the mould and cook in the oven for 50 minutes to 1 hour, until the fruit custard has turned golden.
4. Remove the dish from the oven and leave to cool before sprinkling with the remaining 15ml (1 tbls) of vanilla sugar. You may serve this dessert straight away, or leave it to cool completely and serve very cold. You should not unmould it.

Gâteau-Truffe au Chocolat Noir

Chocolate Truffle Cake

*Serves 6-8. Preparation: 20 min
Cooking: 2 hr the day before serving*
★★

○ **250g (9 oz) bitter chocolate, in pieces**
○ **250g (9 oz) softened butter**
○ **250g (9 oz) caster sugar**
○ **4 eggs**
○ **15ml (1 tbls) flour**

1. Put the chocolate in a bowl over a saucepan of water placed over a low heat. Leave it to melt; do not stir the chocolate, and make sure the water in the saucepan does not boil.
2. Meanwhile, preheat the oven to 195°C (375°F; gas mark 5). Break the eggs in to a bowl and sprinkle in the sugar; stir well, then sprinkle in the flour, and beat well until the mixture becomes light in colour. Reserve one knob of butter to grease the mould, and put the rest of the butter in a bowl; beat it well for 5 minutes.
3. Add the butter, a quarter at a time, to the melted chocolate, blending it in well with a spatula. Then add the egg mixture, stirring all the time.
4. Grease a non-stick charlotte mould 18cm (7 inches) in diameter with the knob of butter, or line an ordinary mould with greaseproof paper. Pour in the mixture, cover with a sheet of foil or a lid, and place the mould in a *bain-marie*. Cook in the oven for 2 hours. Make sure that the water in the *bain-marie* does not evaporate during cooking; if it does, add some boiling water.
5. After 2 hours, remove the cake from the oven and leave it to cool completely (for at least 3 hours) before unmoulding. Once removed from the mould, place the cake in the refrigerator. Serve the next day, or the day after – it is even better then!

This cake is a real delicacy for all who love chocolate and it should be soft and melting in the mouth. A complete dessert as it is, you may also serve it with an egg custard sauce flavoured with vanilla (if you like, you can stir some whipped cream into this).

You can also ice it. Melt 100g (4 oz) of plain chocolate with 30ml (2 tbls) of very strong coffee and 50g (2 oz) of butter; mix together well. Place the cake on a wire rack and spread the icing all over the top. Wait until it cools before serving.

Framboises en Clafoutis

Raspberry Pudding

Serves 6. Preparation: 10 min Cooking: 40 min
★

○ **400g (14 oz) raspberries**
○ **350g (12 oz) single cream**
○ **15ml (1 tbls) flour**
○ **2 eggs**
○ **2 egg yolks**
○ **130g (5¼ oz) sugar**
○ **25g (1 oz) vanilla sugar**
○ **25g (1 oz) butter**

1. Set the oven to 187°C (362°F; gas mark 4½). Mix the vanilla sugar with the sugar. Grease a fireproof porcelain mould or flan dish 22cm (8½ inches) in diameter with some butter and sprinkle in 30ml (2 tbls) of the sugar. Lay the raspberries on top.
2. Put the eggs and egg yolks in a bowl. Reserve 30ml (2 tbls) of the sugar and sprinkle the rest on to the eggs, beating thoroughly until the mixture turns pale. Then add the sifted flour. Mix well, and add the cream, beating for 1 minute. Pour the mixture into the mould over the raspberries and cook in the oven for 40 minutes.
3. At the end of this time, the *clafoutis* should be firm and have puffed up and turned slightly golden. Remove from the oven and leave to cool. Then sprinkle with the remaining 30ml (2 tbls) of sugar. Serve warm or cold.

Clafoutis
Cherry Pudding

Serves 6. Preparation: 15 min Cooking: 40 min

★

○ **750g (1 lb 10 oz) very ripe black cherries**
○ **75g (3 oz) softened butter**
○ **150g (6 oz) caster sugar**
○ **2 eggs**
○ **1 egg yolk**
○ **250ml (9 fl oz) milk**
○ **75g (3 oz) flour**
○ **25g (1 oz) vanilla sugar**
○ **pinch salt**

1. Set the oven at 205°C (400°F; gas mark 6). Wash the cherries and take off the stalks, but do not stone them – this is the traditional way for *clafoutis*.
2. Butter an ovenproof porcelain flan dish or mould, large enough to contain a single layer of all the cherries placed next to each other.
3. Arrange the cherries in the mould, then prepare the pudding mixture: put the eggs and egg yolk in a bowl, sprinkle in the sugar and the pinch of salt. Beat well until the mixture turns pale.
4. Soften the butter in a saucepan over a low heat and add it to the ingredients in the bowl. Mix well before sprinkling in the flour. Pour in the milk and beat until the mixture is smooth and well-blended. Then pour over the cherries. Cook in the oven for 40 minutes.
5. Once cooked, leave the *clafoutis*, or cherry pudding, to cool a little, then sprinkle with the vanilla sugar. Serve warm in the cooking dish.

Flans d'Abricots au Vin Muscat
Apricot Ramekins with Muscat Wine

Serves 6. Preparation: 15 min Cooking: 45 min 4 hr before serving

★★

○ **200g (7 oz) dried apricots or**
○ **300g (11 oz) halved apricots, fresh or tinned**
○ **200ml (7 fl oz) muscat wine**
○ **100g (4 oz) caster sugar**
○ **2 eggs**
○ **2 egg yolks**

1. If using dried apricots, soak them overnight in cold water, then put them through the fine mesh of a vegetable mill or in the blender: if using tinned apricots, drain off the syrup before putting them through the mill or blender, together with 15ml (1 tbls) of the syrup. By either method, you should finish up with 300g (11 oz) of puréed apricots. If you are using fresh fruit, you will need approximately 500g (18 oz) for the same amount of purée. As fresh apricots can be sharp, poach them for 15 minutes in a syrup made from ⅓ litre (11 fl oz) of water and 100g (4 oz) of sugar. Break 3 of the apricot stones and remove the kernels. If you chop or crush these well and add to the custard, they will flavour it deliciously!
2. Set the oven to 195°C (375°F; gas mark 5). Beat the eggs and egg yolks in a bowl together with the sugar; add the apricot purée and stir in the wine. Mix together well for 1 minute, then pour the mixture into 6 ramekins. Place in a *bain-marie* and cook in the oven for approximately 45 minutes until the surface of the custard is firm and springy to the fingertips. Make sure the water in the *bain-marie* does not boil.
3. When cooked, remove the ramekins from the oven and leave to cool. Place them in the refrigerator for at least 4 hours before serving.

Serve with macaroons. If you like, you can flavour the custard with vanilla essence or grated lemon peel. Fresh peaches (not tinned ones) may be used instead of apricots, but in this case a dry white wine should replace the muscat wine.

Remember that the butter in desserts and puddings should be unsalted (English butter is usually slightly salted). Try to use a good quality French Normandy butter wherever possible.

Clafoutis ▶

Île aux Pommes

Floating Island with Apples

Serves 6-8. Preparation and cooking: 1 hr 30 min
30 min before serving
★ ★

For the island, or soufflé:
○ **1kg (2¼ lb) well-flavoured apples**
○ **5 egg whites**
○ **80g (3¼ oz) caster sugar**
○ **20g (¾ oz) butter**
○ **pinch salt**

For the custard:
○ **5 egg yolks**
○ **¾ litre (27 fl oz) milk**
○ **1 vanilla pod**
○ **100g (4 oz) sugar**

1. Set the oven to 220°C (425°F; gas mark 7). Split the vanilla pod in two lengthways. Put in the milk in a saucepan and bring to the boil. Turn the heat off and leave for about 10 minutes.
2. Peel, core and slice the apples. Layer them in an ovenproof dish and cook in the oven, covered, for 30 minutes.
3. Meanwhile, prepare the custard. Separate the eggs, putting the whites in a large bowl together with the salt. Put the egg yolks in a saucepan and sprinkle in 100g (4 oz) of sugar. Beat well until the mixture has turned pale and frothy. Slowly pour in the warm milk with the vanilla pod. Cook the custard over a low heat, stirring continuously, until it coats the back of a spoon smoothly. Remove from the heat and strain through a fine sieve into a bowl. Leave to cool, stirring from time to time, then refrigerate.
4. Butter a mould or sandwich tin 22cm (8½ inches) in diameter and sprinkle in 15ml (1 tbls) of sugar, tilting the mould with your hands so that the sugar adheres evenly to the butter.
5. When the apples have cooked for 30 minutes, remove from the oven and reduce the heat to 195°C (375°F; gas mark 5). Purée the apples in a mill or blender, then stir in half the caster sugar. Sprinkle the egg whites with salt and beat until they are beginning to turn stiff. Then fold in the rest of the sugar, using a spatula. Fold in the apple purée carefully. Pour into the mould. Flatten the surface of the soufflé with the spatula (you can decorate it with a pattern of lines or circles if you like). Place in a *bain-marie* and cook in the oven for 45 minutes.
6. When it is cooked, remove from the oven and leave to cool in the mould for at least 25 minutes. Then turn it out, first on to a wire rack covered with muslin, and then on to a round, slightly hollow serving dish. The soufflé will sink lightly when cooling.
7. Pour the custard sauce around the soufflé just before serving.

This dessert is smooth and extremely light. You should try to use apples that have a lot of flavour and are firm and of the best quality.

Vanilla pods are the fruit of the vanilla orchid. Split the pod in half lengthways before leaving it to infuse in a warm liquid such as milk. Make sure that you squeeze and press the pod so that all the tiny seeds that contain the aromatic substances are released into the liquid. The vanilla pod is very highly flavoured and, even after being warmed or steeped for 10 to 20 minutes in milk, creams or custards, it still retains some of its flavouring. If you rinse and dry the pod you can then keep it in a jar of sugar, which will take on the aroma and be used to flavour other puddings and desserts. You can also buy vanilla as a liquid essence or in powder form.

Île aux **Pralines**

Floating Island with Pralines

Serves 5-6. Preparation and cooking: 30 min
2 hr before serving
★ ★

○ **6 eggs**
○ **275g (10 oz) caster sugar**
○ **¾ litre (27 fl oz) milk**
○ **1 vanilla pod**
○ **2 pinches salt**
○ **24 pralines (candied almonds)**

1. With a sharp knife, split the vanilla pod in 2 lengthways. Put in a saucepan with the milk and bring to the boil. Turn the heat off and cover with a lid. Leave to infuse.
2. Separate the eggs, putting the whites in a bowl and sprinkling with salt. Put the yolks in a saucepan, sprinkle in 75g (3¼ oz) of sugar and stir well with a spatula until the mixture turns pale and frothy. Then pour in the milk, slowly at first to blend the ingredients, and then quickly. Place the saucepan over a low heat and cook until the custard thickens and coats the back of a spoon evenly. Do not let the custard boil. When cooked, strain it through a sieve into a bowl and leave to cool (place the bowl in cold water), stirring from time to time.
3. Put the rest of the sugar in a small saucepan with 45ml (3 tbls) of water over a medium heat. Beat the egg whites until they are just stiff. After the sugar has cooked gently for 5 minutes, check whether you obtained the right consistency of caramel by dropping a little of the syrup into cold water. If it sinks to the bottom and forms a small lump, it is cooked. By that time, the egg whites should be stiff. Slowly pour the syrup onto the meringue mixture, beating continuously, until the ingredients are cold. With an electric beater, beat for another 5 minutes. Meanwhile, crush the pralines, using a pestle and mortar.
4. Now add three-quarters of the crushed pralines (keep the rest for garnishing) to the egg whites, mixing them in with a spatula. Wet a mould or sandwich tin 20cm (8 inches) in diameter; shake off the excess water but do not dry it. Turn the mixture into the mould, flattening the surface with a spatula, and refrigerate for 1 hour. You should also refrigerate the custard, once it has cooled.
5. Just before serving, turn out the soufflé in a deep serving dish and pour the custard around. The soufflé should float like an island. Sprinkle with the remaining pralines and serve.

This dessert should not be served more than 4 hours after being made.

Île aux **Ananas**

Floating Island with Pineapple

Serves 4-5. Preparation and cooking: 30 min
1 hr before serving
★ ★

○ **5 pineapple slices (tinned in syrup)**
○ **4 egg whites**
○ **100g (4 oz) caster sugar**
○ **70g (3 oz) ground almonds**

For the custard:
○ **4 egg yolks**
○ **60g (2½ oz) sugar**
○ **25g (1 oz) vanilla sugar**
○ **½ litre (18 fl oz) milk**

1. Set the oven to 205°C (400°F; gas mark 6). Drain the pineapple on kitchen paper and cut each slice across in halves.
2. Beat the egg whites until just stiff, then add 100g (4 oz) caster sugar and the ground almonds, folding them in as lightly as possible with a spatula.
3. Arrange the pineapple slices on the bottom of a mould and pour over the meringue mixture. Cook in a *bain-marie* for 20 minutes in the oven. Meanwhile, prepare an egg custard sauce, following the recipe on page 9.
4. When cooked, remove the soufflé from the oven and turn out in to a deep dish. Surround with the custard and serve at once, or refrigerate for 1 hour.

Oeufs à la Neige Caramélisés

Snow Eggs with Caramel

Serves 6. Preparation and eooking: 45 min
1 hr before serving
★ ★

- ○ **1 litre (1¾ pints) milk**
- ○ **1 vanilla pod**
- ○ **8 eggs**
- ○ **150g (6 oz) caster sugar**
- ○ **2 pinches salt**

For the caramel:
- ○ **100g (4 oz) caster sugar**

1. With a sharp knife, split the vanilla pod in half lengthways. Put with the milk in a saucepan and bring to the boil. Turn the heat off, cover with a lid, and leave to infuse.
2. Separate the eggs, putting the whites in a large bowl and sprinkling with salt. Put the yolks in a saucepan (enamelled or stainless steel) and sprinkle in the sugar (keeping back 30ml (2 tbls) which will be added to the egg whites). Beat the yolks and sugar together until they turn pale and frothy. Slowly pour in some of the milk, stirring continuously, and when the ingredients are well blended, pour in the rest quickly. Place the saucepan over a low heat. Cook, stirring all the time, until the custard thickens and coats the back of a spoon evenly. Strain through a sieve into a bowl, and leave to cool, placing the bowl in cold water and stirring the custard from time to time.
3. Beat the egg whites until very stiff, then whisk in 30ml (2 tbls) of sugar and continue beating for 1 minute. Meanwhile, fill a large pan three-quarters full of water and bring to the boil. Reduce the heat and let the surface of the water just shiver.
4. Plunge a long-handled ladle into cold water, then pick up a spoonful of the meringue mixture and slide into the water, hitting the handle of the ladle sharply on the edge of the pan to release the mixture. Plunge the ladle into cold water before picking up another spoonful – this will make it much easier to slip off into the water. Spoon out 3 to 6 spoonfuls of the meringue mixture as quickly as possible. After 30 seconds, turn over each little 'island' or ball, using a slotted spoon, and cook for another 30 seconds. Then lift them out and place on a wire rack covered with muslin. Make sure that each 'island' does not come into contact with the others in the water, and when cooked, arrange them wide apart.
5. When the custard has cooked, pour it into a glass bowl and delicately place the meringue balls or 'snow eggs' on top. Prepare the caramel. Put 100g (4 oz) caster sugar with 30ml (2 tbls) of water in a small saucepan. Cook until it turns golden and slowly trickle the caramel over the meringues. Serve at once.

Unless the kitchen is very warm, it should not be necessary to refrigerate this dish. The caramel should always be prepared at the last moment, so that it does not have time to melt the meringue.

Because icing sugar is extremely fine and light, it tends to settle in the packet and become lumpy – and so you must always sift it before giving soufflés, pancakes, and fritters a light dusting of sugar. The best way is to use a cylindrical metal sifter with a pierced lid which will ensure that the icing sugar is spread evenly and lightly.

Mousse au Chocolat au Whisky

Chocolate Mousse with Whisky

Serves 6. Preparation: 15 min
3 hr before serving
★

○ **250g (9 oz) fondant chocolate**
○ **6 eggs**
○ **30ml (2 tbls) scotch whisky**
○ **pinch salt**

1. Put 15ml (1 tbls) of water in a small saucepan and break in the chocolate. Put in a *bain-marie* (or use a double saucepan) and leave to melt over a gentle heat. The water should just shiver.
2. Meanwhile, separate the eggs. Keep the yolks on one side, and put the whites in to a large bowl. Sprinkle with salt, and whisk until just stiff.
3. When the chocolate has melted, remove the saucepan from the heat. Stir in the whisky, beating quickly with a spatula, then stir in the egg yolks. Beat until the mixture is smooth and well-blended. Then fold it into the beaten egg whites, lifting the mixture carefully so that the whites are not broken down.
4. Pour the mousse into a large serving dish, or into 6 ramekins, and put in the refrigerator for at least 3 hours before serving.

Serve with sponge fingers, *langues de chat*, wafers, *gaufrettes*, or brandy snaps.

You may use bourbon, cognac or rum instead of the whisky, or even an orange, tangerine or coffee-flavoured liqueur. The mousse can be made the day before.

Mousse Velours

Velvet Chocolate Mousse

Serves 4. Preparation: 30 min
1 hr before serving
★ ★ ★

○ **250g (9 oz) bitter chocolate**
○ **250g (9 oz) chilled double cream**
○ **3 eggs**
○ **80g (3¼ oz) caster sugar**
○ **pinch of salt**
○ **15ml (1 tbls) coffee essence**
○ **4 maraschino cherries**

1. If you own an electric beater, you will find that this recipe is extremely simple and quick to prepare. Put the cream into a large bowl and whisk with the beater until stiff. Put on one side.
2. Separate the eggs, keeping the yolks on one side. Put the whites in a large bowl, sprinkle with salt, and beat until stiff. Fold into the beaten cream, lifting the mixture from the bottom to the top.
3. Stir the coffee essence into the egg yolks. Put the sugar with 100ml (3½ fl oz) of water in a small saucepan and cook over a medium heat until it becomes syrupy. To check whether the caramel is the right consistency, drop a little into cold water: if it sinks to the bottom and forms a marble, the caramel is ready. Pour the warm caramel on to the egg yolks, a little at a time, beating as quickly as possible (preferably with an electric beater) until the mixture starts to froth and doubles in volume.
4. Meanwhile, break the chocolate into pieces and melt in a *bain-marie* (or use a double saucepan). Beat the melted chocolate into the egg yolk mixture; whisk until the mousse is nearly cold.
5. Stop beating and delicately fold in the meringue and cream mixture, using a spatula to lift the mixture carefully. Put in the refrigerator for 30 minutes.
6. Put the mousse in to an icing bag with a star-shaped nozzle. Pipe large dollops into 4 individual glass bowls, making sure that the mousse does not smear the edges. Decorate each one with a maraschino cherry, and refrigerate until serving.

Mousse au Chocolat au Lait

Milk Chocolate Mousse

○ **250g (9 oz) milk chocolate**
○ **½ litre (18 fl oz) chilled double cream**
○ **2 egg whites**
○ **75g (3 oz) vanilla sugar**
○ **30ml (2 tbls) unsweetened cocoa powder**

1. Put 30ml (2 tbls) of the cream in a small pan placed in a *bain-marie* (or use a double saucepan); break in the chocolate and leave to melt slowly over a gentle heat.
2. Put the rest of the cream in a large bowl and whisk until stiff. Beat the egg whites until just stiff, gradually adding the vanilla sugar. Fold the egg whites into the whipped cream as carefully as possible, using a spatula.
3. When the chocolate has melted, remove from the heat, stirring with a spatula. Leave to cool for a while, but not completely, otherwise it will harden. Carefully fold into the meringue and cream mixture.
4. When the mixture is well-blended, spoon into individual glasses. Smooth the surface of the mousse and refrigerate for at least one hour before serving.
5. Just before serving, coat with an even sprinkling of cocoa, or make a pattern on the surface by cutting out a paper stencil in whatever design you want. Place this lightly on the mousse and scatter the cocoa over. When you remove the paper, the pattern will appear!

Instead of the cocoa, or as well as, you can use a sprinkling of ground hazelnuts.

Mousse au Chocolat au Grand Marnier

Chocolate Mousse with Grand Marnier

○ **400g (14 oz) bitter chocolate**
○ **200g (7 oz) softened butter**
○ **8 eggs**
○ **45ml (3 tbls) grand marnier**
○ **30ml (2 tbls) caster sugar**
○ **pinch salt**

1. Break the chocolate into pieces and put in to a saucepan placed in a *bain-marie* (or use a double saucepan), and leave over a low heat.
2. Separate the eggs, keeping the yolks on one side and putting the whites into a large bowl; sprinkle the salt over.
3. When the chocolate has melted, remove the saucepan from the heat and stir well with a spatula until it is smooth. Stir in the softened butter. When the mixture is well-blended, beat in the egg yolks, one at a time, and then add the liqueur, still beating briskly.
4. Beat the egg whites until stiff, gradually adding the sugar a little at a time. Gently fold in the chocolate mixture, using a spatula.
5. Pour the mousse in to a large glass bowl and leave to set in the refrigerator for at least 6 hours before serving.

Serve with small almond biscuits or macaroons. You may use an orange liqueur or a coffee liqueur such as Tia Maria instead of the grand marnier if you prefer.

Sabayon
Frothy Wine Sauce with Marsala

Serves 4. Preparation and cooking: 15 min

○ **4 egg yolks**
○ **80g (3¼ oz) caster sugar**
○ **150ml (5 fl oz) marsala**

1. Place the egg yolks into a saucepan; sprinkle in the sugar and whisk until the mixture turns pale and frothy. Then whisk in the marsala.
2. Put the saucepan in a *bain-marie* (or use a double saucepan) and cook over a low heat (the water should hardly shiver). Beat until the mixture thickens, froths, and triples in volume. Then remove from heat.
3. Pour into cups and serve at once.

Serve with various *petits-fours* and garnish with a dab of crème Chantilly and a glacé cherry. This wine sauce may be served with charlottes, rice puddings or filled cakes. Leave it to cool completely and then pour it over a fresh fruit salad or fruit poached in syrup, such as strawberries, raspberries, peaches, or pears. Sabayon may be prepared with other wines such as port, madeira or sherry, a muscat or a sweet white wine – or even champagne. You can sweeten a dry white wine by adding a little more sugar to the egg yolks and 15ml (1 tbls) of rum, kirsch or maraschino liqueur.

If you want to serve the sabayon chilled in ramekins, you should add 2 sheets of gelatine (dissolved in cold water) or 30ml (2 tbls) of cornflour diluted with the cold wine to the mixture over the *bain-marie*, otherwise it will not set very well. At the end of the cooking you can add 2 stiffly beaten egg whites, to give extra lightness.

Mousse Moka au Pralin de Noix
Coffee Mousse with Walnut Praline

Serves 6. Preparation: 30 min
1 hr before serving
★★★

○ **6 egg yolks**
○ **200ml (7 fl oz) very strong coffee**
○ **120g (4¾ oz) caster sugar**
○ **200ml (7 fl oz) chilled double cream**
○ **2 gelatine sheets**

For the walnut praline:
○ **12 shelled walnuts**
○ **100g (4 oz) caster sugar**
○ **5ml (1 tsp) lemon juice**

1. Place the gelatine in cold water to soften it. Put the egg yolks in a saucepan together with the sugar and whisk, preferably using an electric beater, until the mixture turns pale and starts to froth. Then beat in the coffee, a little at a time. Still beating, place the saucepan in a *bain-marie* (or use a double saucepan) and cook over a low heat. When the mousse lifts into peaks when you take away the whisk or electric beater, add the squeezed gelatine. Remove from the heat and continue beating, but this time with the saucepan placed in cold water. Beat until the mousse has become lukewarm; then leave to cool entirely.
2. Whip the cream and fold gently into the mousse when it is cold. Turn into individual cups and refrigerate for at least one hour.
3. Prepare the walnut praline: put the sugar, 30ml (2 tbls) of water and the lemon juice into a small saucepan and cook over a low heat. Coarsely chop the walnuts. When the sugar has turned golden and is of a syrupy consistency, add the walnuts. Mix well, turning the saucepan over the heat. When the caramel is darker, pour the contents of the saucepan over a marble chopping board or metal tray. Spread with a thick knife and leave to cool. Then chop very finely with a knife.
4. Just before serving, sprinkle the mousse with the finely chopped walnut praline.

Mousse au Jus d'Orange

Orange Mousse

Serves 4. Preparation and cooking: 15 min
1 hr 30 min before serving
★

○ **4 oranges**
○ **15ml (1 tbls) lemon juice**
○ **60ml (4 tbls) caster sugar**
○ **15ml (1 tbls) cornflour**
○ **30ml (2 tbls) orange liqueur**
○ **2 eggs**

1. Separate the eggs, keeping the whites on one side and putting the yolks in a saucepan with 45ml (3 tbls) of sugar. Beat together until the mixture turns pale. Then beat in the cornflour and lemon juice.
2. Squeeze the oranges and strain the juice through a fine sieve. Slowly add to the saucepan, beating it in with a spatula. Place the saucepan over a low heat and cook, still beating. Allow to boil for 1 minute and remove from heat. Then add the orange liqueur.
3. Whisk the egg whites until stiff and sprinkle in the remaining 15ml (1 tbls) of sugar. Beat for another 30 seconds and quickly fold into the warm custard.
4. When the mixture is blended, turn into 4 bowls and leave to cool. Then put in the coldest part of the refrigerator for at least one hour before serving.

Garnish each bowl with a round of orange (do not peel it) that you have poached in syrup for 15 minutes. To add more flavour, grate the peel of two of the oranges and leave to soak in the squeezed juice of all 4 oranges for 1 hour. Then strain through a fine sieve and prepare the mousse in the usual way.

Mousse à la Crème de Marrons

Marron Cream Mousse

Serves 4. Preparation: 15 min
at least 4 hr before serving
★

○ **500g (18 oz) tinned marron purée flavoured with vanilla**
○ **30ml (2 tbls) cocoa cream**
○ **100g (4 oz) butter**
○ **100ml (3½ fl oz) chilled double cream**

For the sauce:
○ **50g (2 oz) powdered cocoa**
○ **50g (2 oz) caster sugar**
○ **20g (¾ oz) butter**

1. Start this recipe the day before – or at least 4 hours before. Cut the butter into pieces and put in a small saucepan placed over a very low heat. Stir the butter quickly with a spatula until it turns creamy but be careful that it does not melt! Then remove from heat.
2. Put the marron purée into a bowl; stir in the cocoa cream and beat briskly with a spatula. Then add the softened butter and beat the mixture until it is well-blended and light.
3. Whip the cream and add to the bowl, gently folding it in to the mixture with a spatula. Refrigerate for at least 4 hours.
4. 10 minutes before serving, put the mousse into an icing bag with a star-shaped nozzle and pipe large dollops into individual bowls, or cups, making sure the mousse does not smear the edges.
5. Prepare the sauce: put the sugar and cocoa in a small saucepan and slowly pour in 200ml (7 fl oz) of water, beating with a small whisk. Allow to boil for 2 minutes; then add the butter, and boil for another minute, still beating with the whisk. Then remove from heat. Trickle 15ml (1 tbls) of the warm sauce on to each helping and pour the rest into a sauceboat.

Serve with *langues de chat* or *petits-fours*. The mousse may be put into the bowls well in advance and left in the refrigerator until needed.

Mousse à l'Ananas

Pineapple Mousse

○ **10 pineapple slices (tinned in syrup)**
○ **15ml (1 tbls) caster sugar**
○ **4 eggs**
○ **250ml (9 fl oz) chilled double cream**
○ **50g (2 oz) vanilla sugar**
○ **15ml (1 tbls) white rum**

1. Reserve 3 pineapple slices for the garnish and cube the rest. Put the pieces in a basin, pour the rum over and leave to soak. Heat the syrup the pineapple was in.
2. Separate the eggs, putting the whites on one side, and the yolks in a saucepan with the sugar. Beat together until the mixture turns pale. Then pour the heated syrup in slowly, stirring with a spatula. Cook gently over a low heat until the custard thickens and coats the back of a spoon evenly. Remove from the heat and leave to cool.
3. Whip the cream, then sprinkle in 25g (1 oz) of vanilla sugar. Beat once more until very stiff. Put a quarter of this cream on one side for the garnish. Whisk the egg whites until stiff and sprinkle in the remaining vanilla sugar. Whisk for another 10 seconds and fold into the whipped cream.
4. Add the cooled custard to the meringue and cream mixture, and then add the pineapple cubes soaked in rum. Mix together well. Pour the mousse into a large bowl or 6 ramekins and refrigerate for at least one hour before serving.
5. Just before serving, decorate with the pineapple slices and pipe on the reserved whipped cream.

If you use a fresh pineapple (weighing 1.2kg/2¾ lb) for this mousse the flavour will be more delicate, but it will take longer to prepare. Cut the peeled pineapple into cubes and keep back one-fifth for the garnish. Put the rest into an electric blender, then strain through a fine sieve – this should give you about ¼ litre (9 fl oz) of juice which you should add to a custard made with the egg yolks and 125g (4 oz) of caster sugar. Serve within 4 hours of being prepared.

Mousse aux Macarons de Nancy

Mousse with Macaroons

○ **⅓ litre (11 fl oz) milk**
○ **4 eggs**
○ **100g (4 oz) caster sugar**
○ **80g (3½ oz) macaroons (preferably Nancy macaroons)**
○ **60ml (4 tbls) kirsch**

1. Bring the milk to the boil. Meanwhile, crush the macaroons with a pestle and mortar or rolling pin.
2. Separate the eggs. Put the yolks in a saucepan; sprinkle about two-thirds of the sugar over them, beating with a spatula until the mixture turns pale. Then slowly pour in the warmed milk, still beating. Place the saucepan over a low heat and stir continuously until the custard coats the back of a spoon evenly. Then remove from the heat.
3. Pour the kirsch over the crushed macaroons. Whisk the egg whites until stiff; sprinkle in the remaining sugar and beat for another minute. First add the macaroons, then the warm custard to the meringue mixture, folding in with a spatula.
4. Pour into a large bowl or 4 ramekins. Leave to cool completely then put in the coldest part of the refrigerator for at least one hour before serving.

The best macaroons for this recipe come from Nancy in northern France. The result is a light and delicate mousse.

Bavaroise aux Fraises
Strawberry Bavaroise

Serves 6. Preparation: 20 min
4 hr before serving
★

○ **350g (12 oz) strawberries**
○ **250ml (9 fl oz) sirop de fraises
   + 30ml (2 tbls)**
○ **250ml (9 fl oz) chilled double
   cream**
○ **4 gelatine sheets**
○ **15ml (1 tbls) lemon juice**
○ **4 drops vanilla essence**

For the mould:
○ **15ml (1 tbls) caster sugar**

1. Place the gelatine in cold water and leave to soak. Whip the cream. Wash and hull the strawberries. Put 100g (4 oz) on one side for garnishing and pass the rest through a mill or blender. Add the lemon juice and vanilla essence, and mix well.
2. Heat 250ml (9 fl oz) of sirop in a saucepan, but do not let it boil. Add the drained gelatine, stir in well, and place the saucepan in very cold water.
3. When it has cooled, stir in the puréed strawberries. When the mixture starts to set, add three-quarters of the whipped cream, keeping the rest in the refrigerator for garnishing. Stir well.
4. Wet a mould, shake out the excess water but do not dry. Sprinkle the sugar over the bottom and sides, and pour in the bavaroise. Refrigerate for at least 4 hours before serving.
5. Just before serving, dip the mould in lukewarm water for 10 seconds – it should slide out easily. Pipe on the reserved cream to decorate. Decorate with strawberries and pour over the remaining sirop.

Bavaroise aux Framboises
Raspberry Bavaroise

Serves 6-8. Preparation: 45 min
4 hr before serving
★★★

For the white cream:
○ **400ml (14 fl oz) double cream**
○ **45ml (3 tbls) caster sugar**
○ **6 gelatine sheets**
○ **30ml (2 tbls) orange liqueur**

For the pink mousse:
○ **400g (14 oz) raspberries**
○ **150g (6 oz) caster sugar**
○ **30ml (2 tbls) lemon juice**
○ **30ml (2 tbls) kirsch or
   maraschino liqueur**
○ **4 gelatine sheets**
○ **200ml (7 fl oz) chilled double
   cream**

To decorate:
○ **200g (7 oz) raspberries**

For the mould:
○ **15ml (1 tbls) caster sugar**

1. Prepare the white cream. Put the gelatine in cold water to soak. Put the sugar with 30ml (2 tbls) of water in a saucepan over a low heat. When the sugar has melted, add the drained gelatine. Remove from heat, and stir in 30ml (2 tbls) of cream. Then add the rest of the cream and the orange liqueur, stirring briskly. Put the saucepan in cold water.
2. Sprinkle a wetted mould with sugar and place in a large bowl filled with cold water and ice cubes. As soon as the white cream starts to set, pour it into the mould and settle the mould in the bowl of iced water so that first the sides and then the bottom are coated with a layer of the cream. As soon as it is adhering firmly and evenly, put the mould in the freezer.
3. Prepare the pink mousse. Put the gelatine in cold water to soak. Melt the sugar in a saucepan over a low heat together with 15ml (1 tbls) of water. Add the gelatine and stir in well. Remove from the heat and leave to cool. Sieve the raspberries or pass through the fine mesh of a mill over the saucepan and briskly beat the purée in with a whisk. Then beat in the kirsch or maraschino liqueur, with the lemon juice. Whip the cream in a bowl and fold into the puréed raspberries. Mix together carefully.
4. Remove the mould from the freezer and pour in the pink mousse. Chill once more in the refrigerator for at least 4 hours.
5. Just before serving, turn the mousse out on to a dish and decorate with raspberries.

You can use strawberries for this bavaroise, or a mixture of both, or other red fruit such as redcurrants. To make it even more delicious, serve with an egg custard sauce flavoured with orange liqueur.

Reinettes à la Neige

Apple Snow

Serves 7-8. Preparation: 40 min Cooking: 30 min
4 hr before serving
★

○ **1kg (2½ lb) apples**
○ **100g (4 oz) caster sugar**
○ **6 gelatine sheets**

1. Set the oven at 220°C (425°F; gas mark 7). Peel, core, and slice the apples and put in an ovenproof dish, covered with a lid, in the oven to cook for 30 minutes.
2. Five minutes before the apples are due to finish cooking, place the gelatine in cold water to soak. Put the sugar in a small saucepan with 45ml (3 tbls) of water. Bring to the boil over a very low heat for 5 minutes, then turn off the heat.
3. Remove the apples from the oven and purée in a mill or blender.
4. Stir the gelatine in to the syrup – it should melt very quickly. Pour into the apple purée and beat with a hand whisk or electric beater for 25 minutes.
5. By now the mixture should have quadrupled in volume. This mousse should be light and airy, and as white as snow. Turn it in to a wetted bowl or mould and refrigerate for at least 4 hours (or even 2 days). Just before serving, turn out on to a serving dish.

You can also serve this dessert in individual cups or bowls (three-quarters full). You won't need to unmould them, and you might try a sweet sauce with them such as an egg custard flavoured with vanilla, kirsch or maraschino liqueur. Or dilute some redcurrant or blackcurrant jelly and mix with half the amount of cream.

A purée of red fruit in season, mixed with a drop of lemon juice and sugar to taste, can be used in this recipe instead of the apples. It is much lighter than an ordinary bavaroise.

Bavaroises can be of two kinds. The first is a cream or custard flavoured with a liqueur of some sort and sometimes with macerated fruit. The second is made of fruit juice or puréed fruit mixed with sugar and whipped cream. Common to both is the gelatine that sets the custard or puréed fruit in the mould. Serve it unmoulded, like a cake. You can use any shape of mould you choose.

There are two ways to make the unmoulding of a bavaroise simple. Either wet the mould first before you pour in the contents. Shake out the excess water but do not dry the mould. Sprinkle some sugar on the bottom and sides and then fill. Or you can lightly brush the mould with almond oil. The more gelatine it contains, the easier it will be to unmould the bavaroise. Run a knife round the edge of the mould, then turn it over on to a serving dish. It will help if you first dip the mould in hot water for 5 to 10 seconds.

If you decide to make the bavaroise in a glass bowl or a deep serving dish (so that you won't need to unmould it) you will need less gelatine (half the quantity given in the recipe). The delicious taste and lightness of the dessert will be enhanced . . . but it won't look as nice!

Bavaroise aux Bananes

Banana Bavaroise

Serves 8. Preparation: 45 min
4 hr before serving
★★

○ **4 ripe bananas**
○ **500g (18 oz) strawberries**
○ **3 egg yolks**
○ **250g (9 oz) caster sugar**
○ **⅓ litre (11 fl oz) milk**
○ **250ml (9 fl oz) chilled double cream**
○ **5 gelatine sheets**
○ **45ml (3 tbls) lemon juice**

For the mould:
○ **15ml (1 tbls) caster sugar**

1. Wash and hull the strawberries. Choose 100g (4 oz) of the smallest and put them in a bowl with 15ml (1 tbls) of lemon juice. Sprinkle with 15ml (1 tbls) of sugar and leave on one side.
2. Bring the milk to the boil. Put the gelatine to soak in cold water.
3. Put the egg yolks in a saucepan and sprinkle in 125g (5 oz) of sugar. Beat until the mixture turns pale. Pour in the warm milk a little at a time and place the saucepan over a low heat. Stir continuously until the custard thickens enough to coat the back of a spoon evenly. Then remove from heat and add the drained gelatine. Strain through a fine sieve into a bowl standing in cold water and leave to cool.
4. Whisk the cream. Peel the bananas and cut into slices. Add 15ml (1 tbls) of lemon juice and purée them with a fork or in the blender.
5. When the custard is cold, stir in the puréed bananas. Whisk in the beaten cream and the strawberries which have been macerating in sugar and lemon juice.
6. Wet a mould and sprinkle in the sugar. Turn the bavaroise into the mould and chill in the refrigerator for at least 4 hours before serving. Liquidize the remaining 400g (14 oz) strawberries with the rest of the lemon juice and sugar. Sieve the purée to remove all the seeds, and chill in the refrigerator.
7. Just before serving, turn the bavaroise out on to a serving dish and pour the puréed strawberries into a sauceboat.

Raspberries or wild strawberries may be used for this bavaroise.

Bavaroise au Cassis

Blackcurrant Bavaroise

Serves 6. Preparation: 30 min
the day before
★

○ **750g (1 lb 10 oz) blackcurrants**
○ **250g (9 oz) sugar**
○ **30ml (2 tbls) crème de cassis (blackcurrant liqueur)**
○ **6 gelatine sheets**
○ **250ml (9 fl oz) chilled double cream**

To decorate:
○ **200ml (7 fl oz) chilled double cream**
○ **25g (1 oz) vanilla sugar**
○ **15ml (1 tbls) blackcurrants**

for the mould:
○ **15ml (1 tbls) caster sugar**

1. This bavaroise should be made the day before. Put the gelatine to soak in cold water. Add the sugar to 100ml (3½ fl oz) of water in a saucepan and cook over a low heat for 5 minutes until it has turned to syrup. Remove from the heat and add the drained gelatine (which should melt immediately). Stir well in and leave to cool.
2. Wash and purée the blackcurrants – you should now have about 300ml (10½ fl oz) of blackcurrant juice. Stir it in to the cooled syrup and strain through a fine sieve. Add the crème de cassis, and stir again.
3. Whip the cream and fold it in to the fruit just as it is beginning to gel, using a spatula.
4. Wet a mould and sprinkle in the sugar. Turn the bavaroise into the mould and refrigerate overnight.
5. The next day, prepare the garnish 5 minutes before serving. Dip the mould in hot water for 10 seconds and turn out on to a serving dish. Make a crème Chantilly with the cream and vanilla sugar and pipe on in a decorative pattern; garnish with the blackcurrants you reserved from the day before.

Bavaroise au Marrons
Bavaroise with Marrons

○ ⅓ litre (11 fl oz) milk
○ 4 egg yolks
○ 100g (4 oz) caster sugar
○ 200g (7 oz) tinned puréed or creamed marrons
○ 100g (4 oz) marrons glacés pieces
○ 300ml (10½ fl oz) double cream
○ 5 gelatine sheets
○ 30ml (2 tbls) rum or cognac

To decorate:
○ 7 or 8 whole marrons glacés
○ crystallized violets

1. Soak the gelatine in cold water. Bring the milk to the boil. Put the egg yolks in a saucepan, sprinkle in the sugar and beat until they turn pale and frothy. Then stir in the warm milk. Cook over a low heat until the custard thickens enough to coat the back of a spoon evenly. Then add the drained gelatine. Stir in well, then sieve the custard in to a bowl standing in cold water.
2. When it has cooled, stir in the rum or cognac and then the puréed marrons, mixing together well. Whip the cream.
3. When it starts to set, stir in the pieces of marrons glacés and the whipped cream.
4. Wet a mould and fill with the bavaroise. Chill for at least 4 hours.
5. Just before serving, dip the mould in warm water for 10 seconds and turn on to a serving dish. Decorate with the whole marrons glacés and with as many crystallized violets as you like.

A hot chocolate sauce goes very well with this dessert. For this you will need: 100g (4 oz) bitter chocolate and 20g (¾ oz) butter, melted together and mixed with 100ml (3½ fl oz) of milk or whipped cream, sweetened with a little vanilla sugar.

Bavaroise au Café
Coffee Bavaroise

○ ⅓ litre (11 fl oz) milk
○ 60g (2¼ oz) freshly ground coffee
○ 5 egg yolks
○ 180g (7¼ oz) caster sugar
○ 5 gelatine sheets
○ ½ litre (18 fl oz) chilled double cream
○ 15ml (1 tbls) coffee beans in liqueur

For the mould:
○ 15ml (1 tbls) caster sugar

1. Bring the milk to the boil in a small saucepan. Stir in the ground coffee, mixing well, then turn the heat off, cover the saucepan, and leave to brew for 10 minutes.
2. Meanwhile, soak the gelatine in cold water. Put the egg yolks in a saucepan, sprinkle in the sugar and beat until they turn pale and frothy. Then slowly pour in the coffee-flavoured milk through a strainer. Place the saucepan over a low heat and cook until the custard thickens enough to coat the back of a spoon evenly. Remove from the heat and add the drained gelatine. Stir in well and strain the custard through a fine sieve in to a bowl standing in cold water.
3. While it is cooling, whip the cream. Reserve about 30ml (2 tbls) for garnishing. As soon as the custard starts to set, gently fold in the whipped cream with a spatula.
4. Wet a mould and sprinkle in the sugar. Fill the mould, and chill for at least 4 hours.
5. Just before serving, dip the mould in warm water for 10 seconds and turn out on to a serving dish. Pipe on the reserved whipped cream to decorate attractively, and garnish with the liqueured coffee beans.

Bavaroise aux Marrons ▶

Blanche-Neige aux Fruits Rouges
Snow-white Dessert with Red Soft Fruits

Serves 6. Preparation: 45 min
3 hr before serving
★

○ **400ml (14 fl oz) milk**
○ **400ml (14 fl oz) chilled double cream**
○ **150g (6 oz) caster sugar**
○ **4 drops vanilla essence**
○ **2 drops bitter almond essence**
○ **6 gelatine sheets**

For the garnish:
○ **300g (11 oz) raspberries**
○ **300g (11 oz) wild strawberries**
○ **400g (14 oz) redcurrants**
○ **150g (6 oz) caster sugar**
○ **30ml (2 tbls) kirsch**

For the mould:
○ **15ml (1 tbls) caster sugar**

1. Soak the gelatine in cold water. Put the milk and sugar in a saucepan and bring to the boil over a medium heat. Then add the drained gelatine (it should melt immediately). Stir in well and leave to cool, standing the saucepan in cold water.
2. Meanwhile, whip the cream. When the milk starts to set, stir in the vanilla and bitter almond essence and beat for 5 minutes to let as much air in as possible. Then fold the whipped cream in gently.
3. Wet a mould, sprinkle in the sugar and fill. Chill in the refrigerator for 3 hours.
4. Make the garnish. Put 150g (6 oz) caster sugar in a saucepan with 100ml (3½ fl oz) of water over a low heat. When the sugar has melted, turn off the heat. Wash the redcurrants and pass through a sieve or mill, over a bowl. Stir in the cold syrup and kirsch. Wash and hull the strawberries and raspberries, and stir into the puréed fruit. Chill in the refrigerator.
5. Turn out the bavaroise on to a deep serving dish. Pour over the red fruit purée and serve at once.

Blanc-Manger
Blancmange

Serves 8. Preparation: 30 min
4 hr before serving
★ ★

○ **1 litre (1¾ pints) double cream**
○ **110g (4½ oz) caster sugar**
○ **25g (1 oz) vanilla sugar**
○ **7 gelatine sheets**
○ **250g (9 oz) sweet almonds**
○ **3 bitter almonds or 3 drops of bitter almond essence**

For the mould:
○ **15ml (1 tbls) caster sugar**

1. Put half the cream in the refrigerator to use later. Soak the gelatine in cold water. Plunge the sweet and bitter almonds in boiling water, drain immediately and rinse under running water. Skin them between your fingers and place in a blender with 45ml (3 tbls) of cream. Blend until the almonds are finely ground, then add the remaining cream a little at a time. Sieve the almond purée through a muslin cloth into a bowl, squeezing the cloth as tightly as possible to extract all the juice. If you are not using bitter almonds, add the bitter almond essence to the purée. Sprinkle in the sugar and stir in well.
2. Put a quarter of the almond purée in a small saucepan and cook over a low heat. Do not let it boil. Then add the drained gelatine (it will melt immediately). Stir well. Add a quarter of what is left in the bowl to the saucepan, stirring continuously with a spatula. Then pour the contents of the saucepan back into the bowl, still stirring. Blend all together well.
3. When the almond cream is starting to set, whip the reserved cream until stiff and sprinkle in the vanilla sugar. Fold into the almond cream in the bowl as gently as possible. Pour the blancmange into a wetted mould sprinkled with sugar and chill for at least 4 hours before turning out.

Accompany this delicious and traditional dessert (the true ancestor of all bavaroises and utterly unlike nursery blancmanges remembered from childhood) with whole or puréed red fruit, or with a compote of black cherries stewed in red wine.

Délice de Chocolat aux Griottes

Serves 10. Preparation: 35 min Cooking: 45 min
the day before
★ ★

Chocolate and Cherry Delight

For the cake:
○ **120g (4¾ oz) softened butter**
○ **180g (7¼ oz) caster sugar**
○ **120g (4¾ oz) flour**
○ **6 egg whites**
○ **5ml (1 tsp) powdered vanilla**
○ **60ml (4 tbls) kirsch or maraschino liqueur**

For the mousse:
○ **500g (18 oz) bitter chocolate**
○ **½ litre (18 fl oz) chilled double cream**
○ **4 egg whites**
○ **75ml (5 tbls) morello cherries in syrup**
○ **45ml (3 tbls) caster sugar**

For the egg custard sauce:
○ **1¼ litre (2¼ pints) milk**
○ **10 egg yolks**
○ **180g (7¼ oz) caster sugar**
○ **1 vanilla pod**

1. You will need 10 whole eggs altogether for the dessert. Separate them and put the yolks in a covered pan (to be used for the custard). Keep 6 of the whites to make the cake, and 4 for the mousse. Prepare the cake. Grease a sandwich tin 20cm (8 inches) in diameter with 20g (¾ oz) of butter. Put the rest of the butter in a bowl with the sugar (keeping back 30ml (2 tbls)) and powdered vanilla. Cream together well until the mixture turns pale, then sprinkle in the sifted flour and mix together. Whisk the egg whites until stiff, sprinkle in the last 30ml (2 tbls) of sugar and whisk again for another minute. Fold one-quarter of this into the mixture, mix well, then stir in the rest of the egg whites, lifting the mixture carefully. Pour into the tin and cook for 30 minutes. Then turn out on to a wire rack and leave to cool completely.

2. Meanwhile, make the egg custard sauce. Put the vanilla pod, split lengthways in half, with the milk in a saucepan and bring to the boil. Sprinkle the sugar on to the 10 egg yolks and beat until they turn pale. Slowly pour on the hot milk and cook until the custard is thick enough to coat the back of a spoon evenly. Strain and leave to cool.

3. Prepare the chocolate mousse. Break the chocolate into pieces in a saucepan, add 100ml (3½ fl oz) of water and leave to melt in a *bain-marie* over a low heat. Do not stir. Meanwhile, whip the cream. Sprinkle in 15ml (1 tbls) of sugar and beat for 30 seconds more. Whisk the 4 egg whites until stiff. Add the remaining 30ml (2 tbls) of sugar and beat for another 30 seconds. Fold gently into the cream lifting the mixture carefully. When the chocolate has melted, remove the saucepan from the heat and smooth the surface with a spatula. Leave to cool. When it is lukewarm, add 45ml (3 tbls) of the meringue and cream mixture, beat vigorously with a spatula, then pour back into the bowl. Gently mix together, lifting the mixture carefully. Add the morello cherries with their juice and mix once more.

4. Prepare the charlotte mould. Mix the kirsch (or maraschino liqueur) with the same amount of water in a deep dish. Use a cylindrical mould or deep cake tin 20cm (8 inches) in diameter. Cut off the top of the cake in a horizontal slice 1cm (½ inch) thick to make a lid, and cut the rest vertically into strips 1cm (½ inch) wide. Dip the pieces in the alcohol and water mixture and line the bottom and sides of the mould with the thin strips. Now pour in the mousse, smooth over the top with a spatula and put on the cake lid. Chill overnight in the refrigerator, with the egg custard sauce.

5. The next day, turn out on to a serving dish. Pour the egg custard into a bowl and bring to the table.

The original charlotte dates from the beginning of the nineteenth century, and consisted of an apple purée baked in a circular mould that had been lined with strips of toasted and buttered bread. When turned out on to a serving dish, the result was a cake that was firm on the outside and soft inside. It was eaten cold with an egg custard sauce or with a sauce of diluted apricot jam.

Nowadays, the name charlotte is given to any kind of cold custard or mousse dessert that has been turned into a mould and lined with sponge fingers, slices of cake, meringues, macaroons or langues de chat – basically, therefore, a bavaroise in biscuit.

Charlotte Doigts de Fée au Caramel
Caramel Charlotte with Meringue Fingers

Serves 6. Preparation: 30 min
3 hr before serving
★★

○ **4 egg yolks**
○ **150g (6 oz) caster sugar**
○ **250ml (9 fl oz) very strong coffee**
○ **6 gelatine sheets**
○ **250ml (9 fl oz) chilled double cream**
○ **25g (1 oz) vanilla sugar**
○ **100g (4 oz) doigts de fée (chocolate- or coffee-coated meringue fingers)**

To decorate:
○ **15 to 20 coffee beans coated in chocolate, or steeped in liqueur.**

1. Soak the gelatine in cold water. Put the sugar in a saucepan with 60ml (4 tbls) of water over a low heat until it forms a golden syrup. Remove from the heat and slowly pour in the coffee, stirring continuously.
2. Put the egg yolks in a saucepan. Beat, slowly pouring in the coffee-flavoured caramel. Place the saucepan in a *bain-marie* over a low heat (the water should just shiver). Continue beating until the mixture has thickened and is three times the volume, then add the drained gelatine. Beat for another minute, then remove from the heat and leave to cool.
3. Whip the cream, sprinkle in the vanilla sugar, and continue whipping until very stiff. Put about 30ml (2 tbls) in the refrigerator.
4. When the mousse is cold and is starting to set, fold in the rest of the whipped cream. Wet a mould or sandwich tin and fill with the mousse to a height of 4-5cm (1¾-2 inches). Smooth the top with a spatula and chill for 3 hours or more.
5. Just before serving, dip the mould in warm water for 10 seconds and turn out on to a serving dish. Surround with the meringue fingers placed edge-to-edge like a wall. Pipe on the reserved whipped cream to decorate attractively and dot with the coffee beans.

Charlotte aux Fruits Rouges
Strawberry and Raspberry Charlotte

Serves 6. Preparation: 45 min
3 hr before serving
★★

○ **500g (1 lb 2 oz) mixed soft fruit: strawberries, wild strawberries, raspberries**
○ **150g (6 oz) redcurrant jelly**
○ **250ml (9 fl oz) milk**
○ **125g (5 oz) caster sugar**
○ **4 egg yolks**
○ **4 gelatine sheets**
○ **250ml (9 fl oz) chilled double cream**
○ **25g (1 oz) vanilla sugar**
○ **60ml (4 tbls) kirsch**
○ **24 sponge fingers**

1. Soak the gelatine in cold water. Melt the redcurrant jelly over a low heat. Bring the milk to the boil.
2. In a saucepan, beat the egg yolks with the sugar and vanilla sugar, then pour in the milk. Cook over a low heat until the custard is thick enough to coat the back of a spoon evenly. Add the drained gelatine, stir in well and strain through a fine sieve in to a bowl standing in cold water.
3. Put 45ml (3 tbls) of kirsch in a deep dish with 90ml (6 tbls) of water. Dip the sponge fingers in this one by one, and line the bottom and sides of a charlotte mould 18cm (7 inches) in diameter with them. Brush with a little melted jelly. Add the remaining kirsch to the rest of the jelly and dip the fruit into it, gently turning the fruit over to coat thoroughly. Place a layer of fruit in the mould.
4. Whip the cream and gently fold in to the custard which should be starting to set. Pour a layer of this mixture on to the fruit, then add alternate layers of the remaining fruit and the custard. Cover with sponge fingers and chill for at least 3 hours. Turn out on to a serving dish.

A purée of red soft fruits, with lemon juice and sugar, will go very well with this summer charlotte. Instead of mixing the fruit, you can use either raspberries or strawberries on their own.

Charlotte à l'Orange

Orange Charlotte

Serves 6-8. Preparation and cooking: 1 hr
4 hr before serving
★ ★ ★

- ○ **4 large oranges**
- ○ **½ litre (18 fl oz) milk**
- ○ **250g (9 oz) double cream**
- ○ **6 egg yolks**
- ○ **220g (8¾ oz) caster sugar**
- ○ **105ml (7 tbls) orange liqueur**
- ○ **15ml (1 tbls) cognac**
- ○ **45ml (3 tbls) sirop de grenadine**
- ○ **5 gelatine sheets**
- ○ **20 to 24 sponge fingers**

1. Soak the gelatine in cold water. Pour the milk into a small saucepan and grate the peel of one orange into it. Bring to the boil, then turn the heat off, and leave to infuse.
2. Put the egg yolks in another saucepan. Sprinkle in 150g (6 oz) of sugar and stir until the mixture turns pale and frothy. Slowly pour in the warm milk, place the saucepan over a low heat and cook, without letting it boil, until it is thick enough to coat the back of a spoon evenly. Then remove from heat and add the drained gelatine, stirring it in well. Strain through a fine sieve into a bowl standing in iced water. Stir in 30ml (2 tbls) of orange liqueur.
3. Whip the cream. Pour 45ml (3 tbls) of orange liqueur into a deep dish with 90ml (6 tbls) of water. Dip the sponge fingers quickly into the liquid, and line the bottom and sides of a charlotte mould 18cm (7 inches) in diameter with them.
4. When the orange custard is starting to set, gently fold in the whipped cream, lifting the mixture carefully. Fill the biscuit-lined mould, trimming off any protruding ends. Cover the mould and refrigerate for at least 4 hours.
5. Prepare the garnish. Cut the peel off the 3 remaining oranges in thin spirals and cut these into julienne strips like matches. Plunge into boiling water and blanch for 1 minute, remove and drain. Put the remaining 70g (3 oz) of sugar with 200ml (7 fl oz) of water in a saucepan and bring to the boil. Add the strips of peel and the sirop de grenadine. Stir, and cook slowly over a low heat for 10 minutes. Then remove from heat and leave to cool. When cold, add the cognac and the remaining 30ml (2 tbls) of orange liqueur. Stir and pour into a bowl. Chill. Place the 4 peeled oranges into a plastic bag in the refrigerator until serving time.
6. Just before serving, peel the white membrane off the oranges. Break into segments and carefully skin each one with a sharp knife. Turn the charlotte out on to a deep serving dish. Decorate with the orange segments. Strain the orange juice and pour over the charlotte. Serve at once.

There is no need always to stick to sponge fingers to line a charlotte: you can use all sorts of biscuits, as we suggest in some of the recipes in this book. And what about cutting a slightly stale sponge cake into thin slices... that can be a really delicious way of using it up!

Cécilia

Rich Lemon Cream Charlotte

Serves 8-10. Preparation and cooking: 2 hr
of which 1 hr 10 min the day before
★★

For the cake:
○ **5 eggs**
○ **1 lemon**
○ **150g (6 oz) icing sugar**
○ **60g (2½ oz) flour**
○ **60g (2½ oz) cornflour**
○ **20g (¾ oz) butter**
○ **100ml (3½ fl oz) white rum**

For the cream:
○ **4 egg yolks**
○ **100g (4 oz) butter**
○ **160g (6½ oz) caster sugar**
○ **3 lemons**

To decorate:
○ **100g (4 oz) cooking chocolate**
○ **4 egg whites**
○ **200g (7 oz) caster sugar**

1. Prepare the cake the day before. Finely grate the lemon peel and add to 15ml (1 tbls) of lemon juice. Separate the eggs, and add the lemon juice and peel to the yolks. Sprinkle in the sugar and briskly beat (preferably with an electric beater) until the mixture has increased three times in volume. Set the oven to 187°C (362°F; gas mark 4½). Sift the flour and cornflour together. Whisk the egg whites until stiff and add 15ml (1 tbls) at a time, alternating with 15ml (1 tbls) of flour/cornflour, to the egg yolks, beating continuously. Stop beating, and add the rest of the beaten egg white all at once; mix until entirely blended. Butter a mould or sandwich tin 20cm (8 inches) in diameter and fill with the mixture. Cook for 45 minutes. Turn out on to a wire rack and leave to cool until the next day.

2. The next day, prepare the lemon cream. Finely grate the lemon peel into a bowl. Squeeze the juice and add to the peel. This should give you about 75ml (5 tbls) of juice. Put the egg yolks in a saucepan with the lemon juice and peel and beat well. Then sprinkle in the sugar and one-third of the butter. Mix together well and place in a *bain-marie* over a gentle heat. Do not let the water boil. Beat the mixture well, using a whisk or electric beater, until the cream thickens: the track of the whisk or beater should remain on the surface of the cream for a few seconds. Remove from heat and strain through a fine sieve into a bowl. Then stir in the remaining butter and beat again, until the mixture is well-blended, for about 1 minute. Leave to cool.

3. Meanwhile, cut the cake into 3 slices across. Mix the rum with the same amount of water, place one slice of the cake on a serving dish and moisten with one-third of the rum/water mixture. Spread with half the lemon cream. Place the second slice on top; moisten it, and spread with the remaining lemon cream. Place the third slice on top and moisten with the remaining rum/water mixture. You may decorate the cake and serve it one hour later, but it is best to chill it for at least 3 or 4 hours before decorating and serving it.

4. To decorate, melt the chocolate, with 30ml (2 tbls) of water in a *bain-marie*. Pour the melted chocolate on to the centre of the cake and spread evenly over the top with a spatula. Beat the egg whites until very stiff. Put the sugar in a small saucepan with 45ml (3 tbls) of water and cook until the syrup is of the right consistency (check by dropping a teaspoon of syrup into cold water. If it hardens and forms a small marble, it is ready). Pour the syrup onto the beaten egg white and continue beating until the mixture is cold: this is an Italian meringue. Fill an icing bag with the mixture and, using a star-shaped nozzle, pipe a border of rosettes round the edge of the cake. The name 'Cecilia' can be piped in the centre of the cake: it is best to use a simple glacé icing for this. Chill until serving time.

Charlottes can be prepared in all sorts of shape of mould, apart from the cylindrical mould (like a deep cake tin) usually associated with them. You can use a simple pudding basin or a fluted mould – even a dome-shaped cheese cover; anything you can think of, in fact.

Soufflé au Grand Marnier

Serves 3. Preparation: 15 min Cooking: 25 min

Grand Marnier Soufflé

★★★

○ 75ml (5 tbls) milk
○ 15g (½ oz) cornflour
○ 60g (2½ oz) caster sugar
○ 20g (¾ oz) butter
○ 45ml (3 tbls) grand marnier
○ 2 eggs
○ 1 egg white
○ pinch salt

For the mould:
○ 15g (½ oz) butter
○ 15ml (1 tbls) caster sugar

1. Set the oven to 200°C (387°F; gas mark 5½). Separate the eggs, putting the yolks on one side. Put the egg whites, plus the extra egg white, in a large basin.
2. Butter the bottom and sides of a soufflé dish 16cm (6 inches) in diameter and 5cm (2 inches) high. Sprinkle in the sugar.
3. Put 30ml (2 tbls) of sugar, the cornflour and cold milk in a saucepan. Mix briskly, using a whisk, and place the saucepan over a medium heat. Bring to the boil, beating with a whisk all the time so that the mixture, which thickens quickly, remains smooth and no lumps appear. When the mixture has thickened sufficiently, and as soon as it starts to boil, remove from the heat. Still beating with a whisk, fold in the butter, then the grand marnier, and lastly the egg yolks. Do not stop beating as you add each ingredient; the mixture should blend together quite quickly.
4. Sprinkle the egg whites with salt and whisk until stiff. Then fold in the remaining 15ml (1 tbls) of sugar and beat for another minute – do not let it get too stiff. Add 15ml (1 tbls) of beaten egg whites to the contents of the saucepan and beat briskly till blended, then pour the contents of the saucepan into the egg whites at one go; fold in carefully.
5. Pour into the soufflé mould and cook for 25 minutes.

Soufflé au Noix Café

Serves 2. Preparation: 20 min Cooking: 22 min

Walnut-Coffee Soufflé

★★

○ 4 eggs
○ 60ml (4 tbls) caster sugar
○ 30ml (2 tbls) finely grated walnuts
○ 15ml (1 tbls) instant coffee

For the mould:
○ 15g (½ oz) butter
○ 30ml (2 tbls) caster sugar

1. Butter a soufflé dish 16cm (6 inches) in diameter, sprinkle in the sugar and shake out the excess.
2. Dissolve the coffee in 30ml (2 tbls) of warm water. Separate the eggs, putting the whites on one side. Sprinkle the sugar on the yolks in a small saucepan and beat briskly (preferably using an electric beater).
3. Set the oven to 205°C (400°F; gas mark 6). Place the saucepan in a *bain-marie* (or use a double saucepan). Stir the dissolved coffee into the egg yolks and sugar and beat (with an electric beater) until it has increased three times in volume. Then remove from heat and beat again until the mixture is nearly cold. Stir in the grated walnuts.
4. Whisk the egg whites until stiff. Add one-third to the saucepan, mix well, and then pour the contents of the saucepan over the rest of the beaten egg whites. Fold in gently, and turn the mixture into the soufflé mould. Cook in the oven for 22 minutes.
5. Remove from the oven and serve at once.

A few tips for cooking successful sweet soufflés. Do not open the oven door for at least 12 minutes; otherwise the soufflé may sink. Do not overcook a soufflé – this, too, will cause it to sink. Wait a few seconds after the soufflé has risen and turned golden and then take it out of the oven. But check first that it is cooked all through: a soufflé that is uncooked in the middle is a disaster as well! After the all-important first 12 minutes, it will be quite safe for you to open the oven door. At any time after this you can check if it is ready by inserting a skewer in the centre – it should come out quite clean and dry.

Soufflé Minute au Cacao

Serves 3. Preparation: 10 min Cooking: 20 min

Quick Cocoa Soufflé

★

- ○ **3 eggs**
- ○ **45ml (3 tbls) caster sugar**
- ○ **15ml (1 tbls) unsweetened cocoa powder**
- ○ **20g (¾ oz) butter**
- ○ **pinch salt**

1. Preheat the oven to 200°C (387°F; gas mark 5½). Butter the bottom and sides of a soufflé dish 16cm (6½ inches) in diameter and 6cm (2½ inches) high, and sprinkle in 15ml (1 tbls) of sugar. Tilt the mould in your hands to spread the sugar evenly, then shake out the excess. Always take care not to smear the butter and sugar coating with your fingers – this may prevent the soufflé from rising properly.
2. Prepare the soufflé. Separate the eggs, and sprinkle the whites with salt. Put the yolks into a bowl, sprinkle in the sugar and beat until the mixture turns pale and frothy. Then beat in the cocoa powder. Whisk the egg whites until just stiff and fold into the yolks, lifting the mixture carefully with a spatula.
3. Turn the mixture into the soufflé mould and cook for 20 minutes in the oven until the soufflé has risen and turned golden – and it should smell quite delicious!

For extra flavour, add the grated peel of half a lemon or orange with a pinch of powdered vanilla to the soufflé mixture.

Even some famous chefs have failed to achieve the perfect soufflé. And yet it is not a miracle – so long as you follow the rules of the game. A soufflé must satisfy two requirements to be counted a success: it must look good, and it must taste good. Sometimes a good-looking soufflé may turn out to contain too much flour and will be disappointingly heavy; and a delicious-tasting soufflé may be flawed by its undistinguished appearance.

There are three basic rules which must be respected. First the egg whites must be beaten only until just stiff and they must be added to the other ingredients in two stages. A little of the beaten egg whites should first be incorporated with the rest, and this mixture should then be returned to the other egg whites. The tricky part comes now! Turning the bowl clockwise, gently fold the mixture in, dividing it into triangular sections with your spatula and lifting from the bottom to the top so that all is smooth and well-blended. You must do it quickly.

Secondly, the soufflé mixture must fill the mould three-quarters full. If you put in too much it will puff up over the rim of the mould, and if you don't use enough it will look as if it has failed to rise properly at all and won't turn an attractive golden colour. The best soufflé moulds are of fireproof porcelain. They should be 5cm (2 inches) high and not more than 18cm (7 inches) in diameter. Small soufflés usually look better. The mould should be generously greased with butter and the bottom and sides evenly coated with sugar. Don't smear the coating with your fingers – you'll prevent the soufflé from rising properly in that spot.

Thirdly, the oven must not be too hot, otherwise the soufflé will cook quickly on the outside and remain liquid at the centre. Nor should it be too cold, as then it will not rise. You need a medium heat to be sure of a well-risen and properly cooked soufflé.

Soufflé au Chocolat

Serves 3. Preparation: 15 min Cooking: 22 min

Chocolate Soufflé

★★

○ **100g (4 oz) cooking chocolate (bitter or fondant) in pieces**
○ **45ml (3 tbls) double cream**
○ **45ml (3 tbls) caster sugar**
○ **2 eggs**
○ **1 egg white**
○ **pinch salt**
○ **20g (¾ oz) butter**
○ **icing sugar**

1. Set the oven to 195°C (375°F; gas mark 5). Put the cream in a small saucepan with 30ml (2 tbls) of sugar and the chocolate pieces and cook gently in a *bain-marie* over a very low heat until melted.
2. Meanwhile, butter the bottom and sides of a soufflé dish 16cm (6½ inches) in diameter and 6cm (2½ inches) high. Sprinkle in the remaining sugar, tilting the dish to line the mould evenly. Shake out the excess sugar.
3. Separate the 2 whole eggs. Put the whites in a bowl with the other egg white. Add the salt and whisk until just stiff.
4. Remove the melted chocolate from the heat and stir until the mixture is smooth, using a spatula. Then mix in the egg yolks, one by one, and add one-third of the beaten egg whites, still stirring. Pour the contents of the saucepan into the remaining egg whites and fold in gently. Turn the soufflé mixture into the dish and cook in the oven for 22 minutes.
5. At the end of this time, the soufflé should have risen and turned golden. Remove from the oven and sprinkle with icing sugar. Serve at once.

If after 22 minutes cooking time, the soufflé still seems liquid inside (you can check with a skewer), continue cooking for a bit longer.

Soufflé au Citron Vert

Serves 3. Preparation: 15 min Cooking: 18 min

Lime Soufflé

★

○ **2 eggs**
○ **2 egg whites**
○ **5ml (1 tsp) cornflour**
○ **pinch salt**
○ **45ml (3 tbls) caster sugar**
○ **25g (1 oz) vanilla sugar**
○ **20g (¾ oz) butter**
○ **icing sugar**

1. Preheat the oven to 212°C (412°F; gas mark 6½). Butter an oval, ovenproof dish 22cm (8½ inches) long and sprinkle with 10ml (2 tsp) of sugar.
2. Separate the eggs, putting all the whites in a large bowl, sprinkled with salt. Add the vanilla sugar and half the remaining sugar to the yolks and beat until the mixture turns pale. Grate the peel of the lime into the bowl and blend the cornflour with 10ml (2 tsp) of the juice; pour into the egg yolk mixture and beat for another 30 seconds.
3. Whisk the egg whites until very stiff. Beat in the rest of the sugar; whisk for 1 minute more. Add 15ml (1 tbls) of the beaten egg whites to the egg yolk mixture. Mix well, then pour back on to the rest of the whites. Fold in gently, lifting from bottom to top.
4. Turn the soufflé mixture into the dish, using a large spoon, and shape into three tall peaks. Cook in the oven for 18 minutes. Remove and sprinkle with icing sugar. Serve.

This way of serving this light soufflé is typically Viennese. It also looks most attractive if you cook it piled on individual flat ovenproof dishes.

Soufflé d'Amandes aux Cerises

Serves 4. Preparation and cooking: 40 min

Almond Soufflé with Cherries ★★

- ○ **500g (18 oz) black cherries**
- ○ **250ml (9 fl oz) red wine, such as a bordeaux**
- ○ **160g (6 oz) caster sugar**
- ○ **90ml (6 tbls) ground almonds**
- ○ **25g (1 oz) vanilla sugar**
- ○ **2 drops bitter almond essence**
- ○ **3 eggs**
- ○ **1 egg white**
- ○ **50g (2 oz) butter**
- ○ **icing sugar**

1. Wash and stone the cherries and put in a saucepan with 100g (4 oz) sugar and the red wine. Bring to the boil and cook for 5 minutes over a medium heat.
2. Set the oven to 200°C (412°F; gas mark 5½). Butter 4 small soufflé dishes 12cm (4¾ inches) in diameter, sprinkling each with 5ml (1 tsp) of sugar. Separate the eggs, and put the yolks in a bowl with the vanilla sugar and half the remaining sugar. Beat until the mixture turns pale and frothy. Whisk the egg whites until very stiff and sprinkle in the rest of the sugar. Beat for another minute, then add the ground almonds and the almond essence. Mix gently with a spatula. Add 15ml (1 tbls) of the egg whites to the yolks. Mix well, then pour back on to the rest of the beaten egg whites and fold in gently with a spatula.
3. Drain the cherries well and divide among the soufflé dishes. Cover with the almond soufflé mixture and cook in the oven for 20 minutes.
4. Meanwhile, reduce the liquid the cherries cooked in to about 200ml (7 fl oz). Pour into a sauceboat. When the soufflés are cooked, remove from the oven and sprinkle with icing sugar. Serve with the sauce.

Soufflé aux Pommes Dorées

Serves 3. Preparation: 25 min Cooking: 30 min

Golden Apple Soufflé ★★

- ○ **1 large cooking apple**
- ○ **80g (3¼ oz) caster sugar**
- ○ **20g (¾ oz) cornflour**
- ○ **125ml (4 fl oz) milk**
- ○ **3 eggs**
- ○ **3 pinches powdered vanilla**
- ○ **15ml (1 tbls) calvados**
- ○ **60g (2½ oz) butter**
- ○ **pinch salt**

1. Peel and slice the apple finely and brown in 20g (¾ oz) melted butter for 2 minutes on each side. Remove from the heat and put on one side.
2. Preheat the oven to 195°C (375°F; gas mark 5). Grease a soufflé dish 18cm (7 inches) in diameter with 20g (¾ oz) of butter and evenly sprinkle in 20g (¾ oz) of sugar.
3. Put the cornflour in a medium-sized saucepan, and slowly pour in the milk, stirring with a whisk until the mixture is well-blended. Then add half the remaining sugar and the vanilla. Place over a low heat and bring to the boil for one minute, stirring continuously; remove from the heat.
4. Away from the heat, add the remaining 20g (¾ oz) of butter and the calvados to the saucepan. Mix well. Separate the eggs, add a pinch of salt to the whites and whisk until they begin to thicken. Add the rest of the sugar, then whisk again until just stiff.
5. Blend the egg yolks one by one with the contents of the saucepan. Then gently fold in the beaten egg whites, lifting the mixture with a spatula. Pour half the soufflé mixture into the mould and arrange the apple slices in concentric circles on top. Pour the remaining soufflé mixture over and cook in the oven for 30 minutes.
6. When the soufflé is cooked, serve immediately.

Hérisson aux Marrons (p53) ▶

Soufflé à la Noix de Coco

Serves 3. Preparation: 15 min Cooking: 25 min

Coconut Soufflé

★★

○ **150ml (5 fl oz) unsweetened coconut milk**
○ **50g (2 oz) grated coconut**
○ **3 eggs**
○ **1 egg white**
○ **20g (¾ oz) butter**
○ **45ml (3 tbls) caster sugar**
○ **25g (1 oz) vanilla sugar**
○ **15g (½ oz) cornflour**
○ **15ml (1 tbls) white rum**

For the moulds:
○ **25g (1 oz) butter**
○ **30ml (2 tbls) caster sugar**

1. Set the oven to 205°C (400°F; gas mark 6). Put the coconut milk and cornflour in a saucepan with 15ml (1 tbls) of caster sugar and the vanilla sugar. Whisk briskly and place over a low heat, beating continuously with the whisk. When the mixture has thickened and forms peaks, remove from the heat. Fold the butter in with the whisk and leave to cool.
2. Meanwhile, butter the bottom and sides of 3 soufflé moulds or ramekins 11cm (4½ inches) in diameter and sprinkle in the sugar, tilting the moulds to line them evenly.
3. Separate the eggs and add the yolks, one by one, to the saucepan,when the contents have cooled, folding in with a whisk. Then add the grated coconut and rum; mix well.
4. Whisk the egg whites and the extra white until stiff, adding the remaining 30ml (2 tbls) of sugar while beating. Add 30ml (2 tbls) of the beaten egg whites to the contents of the saucepan and mix well. Pour all back on to the rest of the egg whites, and fold in carefully using a spatula to lift the mixture. Put the soufflé mixture into the moulds and cook in the oven for 25 minutes. Serve at once.

If you cannot get any unsweetened coconut milk, use instead 200ml (7 fl oz) of milk. Bring to the boil and add 50g (2 oz) of grated coconut. Leave to steep for 20 minutes then pour through a fine strainer, pressing the coconut to extract all the juice. This should give you about 150ml (5 fl oz) of coconut-flavoured milk.

Soufflés d'Abricots au Noyau

Serves 6. Preparation: 15 min Cooking: 15 min

Liqueur and Apricot Soufflés

★★★

○ **250g (9 oz) dried apricots**
○ **120g (4¾ oz) caster sugar**
○ **4 egg whites**
○ **3 small macaroons or 1 sponge finger cut into small squares**
○ **30ml (2 tbls) liqueur de Noyau (almond-flavoured liqueur)**
○ **50g (2 oz) butter**

1. Soak the apricots in cold water overnight.
2. The next day purée the apricots in a mill or blender – you should get about 400g (14 oz).
3. Preheat the oven to 205°C (400°F; gas mark 6). Butter 6 small ramekins or soufflé dishes 12cm (4¾ inches) in diameter and 5cm (2 inches) high. Sprinkle the bottom and sides of each with 5ml (1 tsp) of sugar.
4. Put the remaining sugar in a small saucepan with 30ml (2 tbls) of water. Cook over a low heat until it has formed a thick syrup. Check its readiness by dropping a little in cold water. It should fall to the bottom and form a small marble.
5. Whisk the egg whites until very stiff. Crumble the macaroons well using a pestle and mortar or a rolling pin. Moisten with the liqueur. When the syrup is ready, slowly pour on to the beaten egg whites, still beating to blend; then add the puréed apricots, folding in gently with a spatula. Add the moistened macaroons and mix again. Turn the soufflé mixture into the ramekins.
6. Cook in the oven for 15 minutes. Serve at once.

Hérisson aux Marrons

Marron and Chocolate Hedgehog

Serves 6. Preparation: 30 min (15 min the day before)

★

○ **500g (18 oz) unsweetened marron purée**
○ **100g (4 oz) fondant chocolate**
○ **60ml (4 tbls) caster sugar**
○ **100ml (3½ fl oz) single cream**
○ **50g (2 oz) butter**
○ **25g (1 oz) vanilla sugar**
○ **30ml (2 tbls) rum**

To decorate:
○ **200ml (7 fl oz) chilled double cream**
○ **15ml (1 tbls) icing sugar**
○ **25g (1 oz) vanilla sugar**

1. Beat the marron purée until creamy, using a spatula. Put the sugar, vanilla sugar and cream in a small saucepan and place in a *bain-marie*. Break in the chocolate and leave to melt over a low heat without stirring. Then add the butter, mixing in with a spatula until the mixture is smooth, and next the marron purée and rum. Mix all together well.
2. Wet a cylindrical (deep cake tin) or domed mould, such as a glass cheese cover. Sprinkle in the sugar evenly and fill with the mixture. Smooth the surface with a spatula and chill in the refrigerator until the next day (or even longer).
3. Just before serving, dip the mould in warm water for 10 seconds and turn out on to a serving dish. Whip the cream until stiff, beat in the caster and vanilla sugar and put into an icing bag with a 1cm (½ inch) diameter plain nozzle. Pipe on small raised dots or cones, very close together, to look like the prickles on a hedgehog. Serve at once.

Serve this dessert with a warm chocolate sauce made from 100g (4 oz) bitter chocolate melted in 200ml (7 fl oz) double cream or milk and mixed with 25g (1 oz) butter.

Crème de Patates Douces au Chocolat

Sweet Potato Gâteau with Chocolate Sauce

Serves 6. Preparation and cooking: 55 min (1 hr before serving)

★

○ **1.2kg (2¾ lb) sweet potatoes**
○ **50g (2 oz) vanilla sugar**
○ **250g (9 oz) plain chocolate**
○ **400ml (14 fl oz) milk**

1. Wash the sweet potatoes. Put in a large saucepan, cover generously with cold water, and cook over a medium heat for about 30 minutes. Check whether they are cooked by piercing with a knife. (You can also steam the sweet potatoes.)
2. Drain in a colander and leave to cool for 5 minutes. Then peel, while they are still warm, and sieve into a bowl.
3. Heat 150ml (5 fl oz) of milk with the vanilla sugar. When the sugar has melted, pour the milk on to the sweet potatoes, stirring in vigorously with a spatula.
4. Pour the purée into a deep dish and mould in to the shape of a volcano (or you can use a kugelhopf mould). Leave to cool.
5. Meanwhile, break the chocolate into pieces in a saucepan with the remaining milk and stand in a *bain-marie* (or use a double saucepan) to melt slowly over a low heat. Smooth the surface of the chocolate with a spatula, then remove from the heat and leave to cool for 5 minutes, if necessary by standing in cold water.
6. When it has cooled to lukewarm, pour the chocolate into the crater of the volcano so that it overflows and runs down the outside of the cake, and spreads around the bottom. Leave in a cool place or refrigerator for at least one hour before serving. It should be cold, but not chilled.

You may, if you choose, add more sugar to the purée of sweet potatoes... or else a knob of butter, some cinnamon, or some grated nutmeg. The milk can be replaced by single cream or coconut milk.

Pavé de Marrons aux Noisettes

Marron and Hazelnut Brick

Serves 6. Preparation: 20 min
2 hr before serving
★★

○ **1 tin 400g (14 oz) unsweetened marron purée**
○ **200g (7 oz) softened butter**
○ **4 egg yolks**
○ **100g (4 oz) caster sugar**
○ **100g (4 oz) finely chopped hazelnuts**

1. Put the sugar with 60ml (4 tbls) water in a small saucepan and cook over a low heat. Check whether the syrup is ready by dipping the tip of a teaspoon into it. Remove it from the heat and grip between your fingers. Threads should pull away from the spoon when you lift your fingers.
2. Place the egg yolks into a bowl and beat well. When the syrup is ready, slowly pour it into the egg yolks, beating all the time until the mixture is nearly cold, light and frothy. Add the butter, a little at a time, beating more slowly now.
3. When the butter is well-blended, add the marron purée, spoonful by spoonful, mixing well; then the hazelnuts, and mix once more.
4. Wet a rectangular mould (an ice tray would do well) and shake out the excess water. Fill the mould, pressing the mixture down well and chill in the refrigerator for at least 2 hours before serving. To unmould the brick more easily, dip the mould in warm water for 20 seconds and turn out on to a serving dish.

You can make this dessert even richer by adding chopped crystallized fruit that has been soaked in rum, or raisins soaked in madeira. You can also add 100g (4 oz) of finely grated fondant chocolate. Use fresh chestnuts when they are in season, cooked in milk and puréed. Serve with an egg custard sauce flavoured with vanilla.

Délice de Noix

Walnut Cream Delight

Serves 8. Preparation and cooking: 30 min
4 hr before serving
★★

○ **300g (11 oz) shelled walnuts**
○ **⅓ litre (11 fl oz) milk**
○ **4 egg yolks**
○ **200g (7 oz) caster sugar**
○ **15ml (1 tbls) cornflour**
○ **250g (9 oz) softened butter**
○ **45ml (3 tbls) rum, crème de cacao or coffee liqueur**
○ **icing sugar**

For the sauce:
○ **200g (7 oz) fondant chocolate**
○ **150ml (5 fl oz) coffee**
○ **100ml (3½ fl oz) cream**
○ **25g (1 oz) butter**

1. Keep 9 shelled walnuts for decoration and coarsely chop the rest. Dilute the cornflour in the cold milk.
2. In a saucepan, beat the egg yolks with half the sugar until the mixture turns pale and frothy. Then sprinkle in the remaining sugar and slowly pour in the milk. Place the saucepan over a low heat and cook, stirring continuously until it starts to boil. Allow to boil for one minute, then remove from the heat and stand the saucepan in cold water. Stir until the mixture is lukewarm. Add the liqueur and the butter cut into pieces. Whisk well, then fold in the chopped walnuts.
3. Wet a mould or sandwich tin and fill with the mixture. Chill in the refrigerator for at least 4 hours.
4. 10 minutes before serving, break the chocolate in pieces and put in a saucepan with the coffee and cream. Cook slowly in a *bain-marie* until melted. Turn the gâteau out on to a serving dish. Sprinkle with icing sugar and decorate with the reserved walnuts. When the chocolate has melted, stir in the butter. Mix until smooth with a spatula.
5. Bring the dessert to the table and serve the warm chocolate sauce separately.

Igloo

Coconut Cream Igloo

Serves 4-6. Preparation: 30 min
4 hr before serving
★

- ○ **125g (5 oz) grated coconut**
- ○ **200g (7 oz) caster sugar**
- ○ **250ml (9 fl oz) milk**
- ○ **90ml (6 tbls) cornflour**
- ○ **100ml (3½ fl oz) chilled double cream**
- ○ **25g (1 oz) vanilla sugar**
- ○ **4 drops cinnamon essence**
- ○ **30ml (2 tbls) white rum**

1. Put the sugar in a saucepan with 200ml (7 fl oz) of water. Cook over a medium heat until the syrup starts to boil. Then sprinkle in 100g (4 oz) of grated coconut and cook over a low heat for 10 minutes.
2. Meanwhile, blend the cornflour with the cold milk and place over a low heat. Cook, whisking continuously, until it thickens. Then pour in the coconut-flavoured syrup and cook for another 2 minutes, beating all the time until the mixture is well-blended.
3. Remove from the heat and stand the saucepan in cold water. Whip the cream, add the vanilla sugar and beat again until very stiff.
4. When the coconut mixture is cold, add the cinnamon, rum and whipped cream, beating with a whisk.
5. Wet a cylindrical (deep cake tin) or domed mould such as a glass cheese cover and fill with the mixture. Smooth the surface with a spatula and leave to cool. Then place in the refrigerator for at least 4 hours.
6. Just before serving, turn the gâteau out on to a serving dish covered with white paper. Sprinkle with the remaining 25g (1 oz) of grated coconut and bring to the table.

Serve with a chocolate sauce, either warm or cold, made by melting 100g (4 oz) of chocolate in 200ml (7 fl oz) of milk, together with a knob of butter. The igloo will look even more attractive if you coat it with 150g (5 oz) of crème Chantilly. Or you can cover it with Italian meringue – beat 2 egg whites until very stiff and fold in a hot syrup made with 100g (4 oz) of sugar dissolved in 30ml (2 tbls) of water. Continue whisking until cold. This very white, smooth and light meringue spread over the dome-shaped gâteau will make it look really snowy and realistic.

By far the best sort of chocolate to use in desserts is a really dark and bitter one, because it will be of the highest quality and made from the best cocoa beans and there will be a higher proportion of cocoa to sugar. So, even though it may be more expensive, you will need less of it to get the fullest possible flavour. And you can always sweeten it by adding sugar and milk to taste.

Cooking chocolate (or chocolate de ménage) contains a higher proportion of sugar – 65% sugar to 35% cocoa – and is therefore cheaper. But because it is made from cocoa beans of only medium quality it is much grainier, and cannot be mixed to a really smooth consistency.

Monts Blancs

Serves 6. Preparation: 25 min

Meringues with Marrons and Crème Chantilly

★★

○ **250g (9 oz) marrons glacés, in a paste**
○ **25g (1 oz) softened butter**
○ **15ml (1 tbls) rum**
○ **½ litre (18 fl oz) chilled double cream**
○ **30ml (2 tbls) caster sugar**
○ **25g (1 oz) vanilla sugar**
○ **12 oval meringues**

To decorate
○ **icing sugar**

1. Whip the cream, then sprinkle in the caster and vanilla sugar and beat again until very stiff. Fill an icing bag with a star-shaped nozzle with the crème Chantilly.
2. Take 6 individual bowls or glasses (they should be quite shallow) and pipe a dollop of cream, shaped decoratively into a peak, in each, making sure it does not touch the edge of the bowl. Place 2 meringues on either side, the flat side touching the cream.
3. In a bowl, beat the marron paste with a spatula until smooth, then add the rum and softened butter. Mix again and put into an icing bag with a plain nozzle 0.5cm (⅛ inch) in diameter. Pipe an entwining pattern of vermicelli on to each peak of whipped cream, but do not cover completely.
4. Sprinkle generously with icing sugar before serving.

You can make the flat meringues used in this recipe yourself. Whisk 3 egg whites until very stiff and sprinkle in 150g (6 oz) of caster and icing sugar mixed together. Fill an icing bag with a plain nozzle 2cm (¾ inch) in diameter and squeeze out a circle of meringue on to a greased sheet dusted with flour. Cook in the oven for 1 hour 30 minutes. The heat should be very low – leave the door ajar – and do not let the meringues brown.

You can make one large *mont blanc* for 6 people, instead of 6 individual ones. Mix 500g (18 oz) of marron glacé paste with 60g (2½ oz) butter and 45ml (3 tbls) of rum. Fill an icing bag with the purée and squeeze out fine coils of vermicelli into a savarin mould 22cm (8½ inches) in diameter. Turn out over a large, flat meringue case (or even on to a shortcrust pastry base, or a sponge cake) and fill the centre with 500g (18 oz) of crème Chantilly. Arrange small meringues round the edge of the gâteau, like a crown.

Cocoa beans are the seeds of the cacao tree, native to South America. About fifty of them are embedded in the pinkish pulp of each of its pod-like fruits. The Aztecs and the Mayas called the beans the 'food of the gods'. The beans are fermented, dried and roasted. Then they are broken into small pieces called nibs, and their brittle shells discarded. At this stage, the beans contain 66% fat. They are carefully selected, by quality and flavour, for grinding (the best chocolate is made from a mixture of different beans). Two products are derived from this process: cocoa butter (from the fat content) and dried cocoa powder. This latter, mixed with sugar and butter to a smooth paste, is used to make couverture *chocolate, used for icing desserts and gâteaux.*

Crème de Cerises au Riz Soufflé

Cherry Cream with Rice Crispies

Serves 8. Preparation: 1 hr
4 hr before serving
★★

○ **250g (9 oz) cherries**
○ **250g (9 oz) redcurrant jelly**
○ **250g (9 oz) double cream**
○ **200g (7 oz) fondant chocolate**
○ **100g (4 oz) rice crispies**
○ **100g (4 oz) butter**

To decorate:
○ **Maraschino cherries**
○ **angelica strips**

1. Wash and stone the cherries. Place in a saucepan with the redcurrant jelly and cook over a brisk heat for approximately 10 to 15 minutes. Put a drop of the juice onto a plate; if it sets immediately, remove the saucepan from the heat and leave to cool until nearly cold.
2. Break the chocolate into pieces, put in a saucepan with 30ml (2 tbls) of water and cook in a *bain-marie* over a low heat. When the chocolate has melted, add the butter. Stir well and smooth the surface of the mixture with a spatula. Remove from the heat and sprinkle in the rice crispies. Pour the still warm mixture into a flan dish 24cm (9½ inches) in diameter, spreading thinly over the bottom and more thickly at the sides. Place in the refrigerator to harden the chocolate.
3. When they have cooled, pour the cherries into an electric blender. Blend well, then add the cream, and mix until smooth.
4. Remove the mould from the refrigerator and spread the cherry cream inside the rice crispies. Put back in the refrigerator for at least 4 hours before serving.
5. Just before serving, decorate with the maraschino cherries, arranging the strips of angelica to look like leaves.

Riz au Lait à l'Orange

Rice Pudding with Macerated Oranges

Serves 6. Preparation and cooking: 1 hr
1 hr before serving
★

○ **250g (9 oz) long grain rice**
○ **200ml (7 fl oz) orange concentrate**
○ **750ml (27 fl oz) milk**
○ **10ml (2 tsp) orange flower water**
○ **125g (5 oz) double cream**
○ **pinch saffron threads**
○ **5ml (1 tsp) coarse salt**
○ **6 oranges**
○ **30ml (2 tbls) caster sugar**

1. Bring 1½ litres (2¾ pints) of water to the boil with the salt and saffron. Wash the rice and plunge into the boiling water. Cook over a medium heat until the rice turns golden with the saffron.
2. Meanwhile, bring the milk to the boil. After the rice has cooked for 10 minutes, drain and add to the milk. As soon as it starts to boil again, reduce the heat and cook for approximately 30 minutes, until the rice is very soft. Turn the heat off and leave to cool a little.
3. While the rice is still warm, stir in the orange concentrate and 5ml (1 tsp) of orange flower water. Mix well and leave to cool completely. Meanwhile, peel the oranges. Slice them thinly and moisten with the remaining 5ml (1 tsp) of orange flower water. Sprinkle with sugar and leave in the refrigerator.
4. When the rice is cold, stir in the cream and turn into a bowl. Chill in the freezer compartment until very cold (between 30 minutes and one hour). Serve the rice and the macerated oranges together.

Other fruits may be used for this recipe – strawberries, raspberries, pineapple, tangerines, redcurrants. Flavour the rice accordingly.

Gâteau de Riz aux Trois Parfums

Serves 6-8. Preparation and cooking: 1 hr 35 min
(40 min on the previous day) ★

Three-Flavour Rice Pudding

○ **300g (11 oz) long grain rice**
○ **1¾ litres (3 pints) milk**
○ **250g (9 oz) sugar**
○ **8 eggs**
○ **1 vanilla pod**
○ **peel of 1 lemon, in a thin ribbon**
○ **1 cinnamon stick**
○ **50g (2 oz) butter**
○ **5ml (1 tsp) coarse salt**

1. The day before put 1½ litres (2½ pints) of milk in a large saucepan. Split the vanilla pod in half lengthways and add to the milk with the cinnamon stick and lemon peel. Bring to the boil over a low heat.
2. Wash the rice and blanch for 5 minutes in boiling salted water, then drain in a colander.
3. As soon as the milk boils, add the rice and bring back to the boil. Reduce the heat and cook for 30 minutes. Then turn the heat off and sprinkle in half the sugar and two-thirds of the butter. Leave until the next day.
4. The next day, set the oven to 205°C (400°F; gas mark 6). Beat the eggs together with the remaining sugar, then stir in the rest of the milk. Mix well. Remove the vanilla pod, cinnamon stick and lemon peel from the rice and pour the mixture over. Mix well with a spatula.
5. Grease an ovenproof dish at least 4cm (1½ inches) deep with the rest of the butter. Fill with the mixture and cook in the oven for 45 minutes. After 15 minutes, reduce the temperature to 195°C (375°F; gas mark 5).
6. Leave to cool completely before serving.

Gâteau de Riz aux Deux Liqueurs

Serves 8. Preparation: 50 min
Cooking: 1 hr, the day before ★

Baked Rice Pudding with Two Liqueurs

○ **250g (9 oz) long grain rice**
○ **1½ litres (2½ pints) milk**
○ **200g (7 oz) sugar**
○ **4 eggs**
○ **100g (4 oz) flaked almonds**
○ **100g (4 oz) crystallized orange peel**
○ **1 lemon**
○ **2.5ml (½ tsp) powdered vanilla**
○ **45ml (3 tbls) maraschino liqueur**
○ **45ml (3 tbls) almond liqueur**
○ **2 pinches salt**
○ **30g (1¼ oz) butter**

1. Put the milk with one pinch of salt and half the sugar into a large saucepan. Bring to the boil over a low heat, stirring frequently to dissolve the sugar. Wash the rice, and throw into the milk as soon as it boils. Cook over a low heat for 30 minutes, remove from the heat and leave to cool.
2. Meanwhile, set the oven to 200°C (387°F; gas mark 5½). Butter a high-sided flan dish 26cm (12 inches) across. Brown the almonds over a medium heat, shaking the pan from time to time. Dice the orange peel.
3. Separate the eggs, putting the whites, sprinkled with the rest of the salt, in a large bowl. Add the remaining sugar and the powdered vanilla to the yolks and beat until the mixture turns pale. Then grate in the lemon peel and stir in the still warm rice, mixing vigorously. Crumble the almonds and add, with the crystallized orange peel, to the mixture. Whisk the egg whites until stiff and gently fold into the rice mixture.
4. Fill the flan dish with the mixture and cook in the oven for one hour. Then leave to cool completely.
5. When it is cold, prick all over and pour over the liqueurs, one after the other. Leave until the next day.

Riz au Miel et à la Cannelle

Serves 5-6. Preparation and cooking: 1 hr

Rice Pudding with Honey and Cinnamon

★

- ○ **1 litre (1¾ pints) milk**
- ○ **150g (6 oz) pudding rice**
- ○ **50g (2 oz) caster sugar**
- ○ **100g (4 oz) honey**
- ○ **10ml (2 tsp) powdered cinnamon**
- ○ **pinch salt**

1. Bring the milk to the boil with the salt and sugar.
2. Wash the rice well and sprinkle in to the boiling milk. Bring back to the boil, reduce to a very low heat and cook, without stirring, for about 45 to 50 minutes, until the rice is very soft.
3. Now remove from the heat and stir in the honey. Pour into a deep dish or into individual bowls. Sprinkle with cinnamon – in a pattern if you want to, or use a paper stencil cut to a design of your own choosing.
4. Serve at once, or leave to cool completely before chilling in the refrigerator for 2 hours.

You can give this rice pudding an oriental flavour by adding 30ml (2 tbls) of grilled sesame seeds, almonds, ground pistachio nuts, or even sultanas. Flavour the milk with cloves, vanilla and ginger and serve with a dash of rose water.

Gâteau de Riz Meringué au Caramel

Serves 6-8.
Preparation and cooking: 1 hr 30 min

Caramel Rice with Custard

★

- ○ **200g (7 oz) long grain rice**
- ○ **750ml (27 fl oz) milk**
- ○ **200g (7 oz) caster sugar**
- ○ **5 egg whites**
- ○ **30g (1¼ oz) butter**
- ○ **peel of ½ lemon**
- ○ **100g (4 oz) mixed dried fruit**
- ○ **2 pinches salt**

For the custard:
- ○ **5 egg yolks**
- ○ **750ml (27 fl oz) milk**
- ○ **100g (4 oz) sugar**
- ○ **30ml (2 tbls) rum**

1. Prepare the rice. Split the vanilla pod in half lengthways and put in a saucepan with the milk, one pinch of salt, and the peel of half a lemon. Bring to the boil. Wash the rice well and sprinkle in to the milk as soon as it boils. Bring back to the boil, reduce to a very low heat and cook for 30 minutes.
2. Preheat the oven to 200°C (387°F; gas mark 5½). When the rice has cooked, turn the heat off, removing the lemon peel and vanilla pod. Stir in half the sugar, the butter and dried fruit. Mix well. Whisk the egg whites until stiff (having added the remaining salt) and fold in to the warm rice, lifting the mixture with a spatula.
3. Put the rest of the sugar with 30ml (2 tbls) of water in a charlotte mould of 2 litre (3½ pints) capacity. Place over a medium heat. When the sugar turns golden, tilt the mould in your hands to coat the bottom and sides evenly with the caramel. Then pour in the rice pudding, smoothing the surface with a spatula. Cook in a *bain-marie* in the oven for 40 minutes.
4. Meanwhile, prepare the custard following the recipe on page 9. Leave to cool, then stir in the rum and chill in the refrigerator.
5. When the rice pudding is cooked (a skewer inserted into the centre should come out completely clean and dry), remove from the oven and leave for 10 minutes before turning out in to a deep dish.

This dessert can be served slightly warm, with the custard chilled – but it is quite as good hot as it is cold!

Semoule aux Poires Sauce Chocolat

Serves 6. Preparation and cooking: 50 min (3 hr before serving) ★

Semolina and Pears with Chocolate Sauce

○ **900g (2 lb) pears (6 small ones or 3 large ones)**
○ **150g (6 oz) very fine semolina**
○ **150g (6 oz) caster sugar**
○ **50g (2 oz) vanilla sugar**
○ **250g (9 oz) single cream**
○ **30ml (2 tbls) rum (optional)**

For the sauce:
○ **150g (6 oz) fondant chocolate**
○ **200ml (7 fl oz) milk**
○ **30g (1 oz) butter**

1. If the pears are small, peel them, leaving the stalks on. If they are large, cut in half, peel and remove the stalk and core.
2. Bring 1 litre (1¾ pints) of water to the boil over a medium heat with the caster and vanilla sugar. Cook the pears in this syrup for 15 to 30 minutes. When the tip of a knife pierces them easily, drain them and place in a bowl, moistened with a little of the syrup they cooked in.
3. You will need about three-quarters of a litre (1¼ pints) of this syrup to make the semolina. Make up the rest with water. Bring the syrup to the boil, sprinkle in the semolina, stirring with a spatula, and cook over a low heat for 15 minutes, still stirring all the time. After 12 minutes, slowly pour in the cream. Add the rum away from the heat and mix well.
4. Wet a savarin or ring mould, and fill with the warm semolina; smooth the surface with a spatula and leave to cool. Put the pears and the semolina pudding in the refrigerator for 3 hours.
5. 10 minutes before serving, turn the semolina pudding out on to a serving dish and place the pears in the centre. Make the sauce by adding the chocolate pieces to the boiling milk in a saucepan and leaving to melt over a low heat. Then stir the butter in quickly with a spatula. When the sauce is smooth, remove from the heat and pour a little over the pears. Serve the rest in a sauceboat.

Gâteau de Semoule aux Raisins

Serves 6-8. Preparation and cooking: 50 min 1 hr before serving ★

Semolina Pudding with Sultanas

○ **1½ litres (barely 2½ pints) milk**
○ **1 vanilla pod split in half**
○ **4 eggs**
○ **90ml (6 tbls) fine semolina**
○ **115ml (9 tbls) sugar**
○ **100g (4 oz) sultanas**
○ **45ml (3 tbls) rum or kirsch**

For the caramel:
○ **60ml (4 tbls) sugar**

1. The day before, wash the sultanas and leave to soak in the rum or kirsch.
2. The next day, bring the milk to the boil together with the vanilla and sugar. Then remove from the heat and leave to infuse.
3. Prepare the caramel. Put the sugar and 30ml (2 tbls) of water in a small saucepan and cook over a medium heat until a golden syrup is formed. Pour this into a brioche or charlotte mould of 1½ litre (2½ pints) capacity. Tilt the mould in your hands to coat the bottom and sides of the mould evenly with the caramel.
4. Separate the eggs, putting the whites in a large bowl. Whisk until stiff.
5. Put 1 litre (1¾ pints) of the flavoured and sweetened milk in a saucepan and bring to the boil. Sprinkle in the semolina and cook for approximately 8 minutes, stirring continuously. Then fold in the beaten egg whites and cook for another 2 minutes, still stirring. Add the sultanas, mix well and remove from heat.
Turn the rice pudding into the caramelized mould. Pat firmly down, and smooth the top of the pudding with a spatula. Leave to cool.
6. Meanwhile, prepare a custard sauce with the egg yolks and remaining milk, following the instructions given on page 9. Leave to cool.
7. When the pudding and custard are cold, serve together; or chill in the refrigerator for a few hours more.

Semoule aux Poires Sauce Chocolat ▶

Pain Perdu

Serves 4. Preparation: 10 min Cooking: 10 min

French Toast

★

○ **8 slices white bread**
○ **125g (5 oz) butter**
○ **100g (4 oz) granulated sugar**
○ **250ml (9 fl oz) milk**
○ **4 eggs**
○ **25g (1 oz) vanilla sugar**

1. Clarify the butter: place it in a small saucepan and cook slowly until a residue forms and sinks to the bottom. Remove from the heat and strain off the clear yellow liquid above to use for the frying.
2. Bring the milk to the boil, with the sugar and vanilla sugar. Pour into a basin.
3. Beat the eggs well in another basin.
4. Slowly pour half the clarified butter into a frying pan large enough to hold 4 slices of bread, placed over a medium heat. Quickly dip each slice of bread first in the milk and then in the beaten egg yolks, making sure both sides are covered. Then put into the hot butter. Fry on one side, then turn over. It should take about 3 to 4 minutes. Remove the bread with a spatula and place on a serving dish. Pour in the rest of the clarified butter, and fry the rest of the bread. Serve at once.

You may sprinkle the bread with sugar and serve it with apple purée or apricot jam.

Gâteau de Pain Blanc aux Cerises Noires

Serves 6-8. Preparation: 35 min Cooking: 45 min

White Bread Pudding with Black Cherries

★

○ **one 250g (9 oz) brioche type loaf**
○ **1kg (2¼ lb) black cherries**
○ **1 litre (1¾ pints) boiled milk**
○ **200g (7 oz) caster sugar**
○ **5 eggs**
○ **60g (2¼ oz) softened butter**
○ **45ml (3 tbls) kirsch**
○ **2.5ml (½ tsp) powdered vanilla**

1. For this recipe you will need to use an ovenproof gratin dish or a porcelain flan dish that is large enough to hold the cherries in a single layer.
2. Cut the bread into slices 1cm (½ inch) thick to line the bottom of the mould. Keep them on one side for the time being.
3. Wash and stone the cherries, put in a large bowl and pour over the kirsch. Sprinkle with 45ml (3 tbls) of sugar.
4. Butter the dish. Spread the slices of bread thinly with butter on both sides. Brown slightly on both sides under the grill and arrange in the dish. Place the cherries in their juice on top.
5. Heat the milk, without boiling. Break the eggs into a bowl and sprinkle in the sugar. Whisk until the mixture turns pale and frothy. Then add the vanilla and warm milk, a little at a time, stirring continuously. Pour this mixture slowly over the cherries in the dish, holding the bread down with a slice. Wait for 5 minutes while the bread soaks up the liquid. Meanwhile, set the oven to 200°C (387°F; gas mark 5½).
6. Bake in the oven for 45 minutes or more, until the custard sets. Serve hot in the cooking dish.

Accompany with redcurrant jelly thinned with a little hot water and flavoured with 45ml (3 tbls) of kirsch.

Gâteau de Pain Beurre à l'Anglaise

English Bread and Butter Pudding

*Serves 8. Preparation: 25 min
(30 min before cooking) Cooking: 1 hr*
★

- ○ **18 slices white bread**
- ○ **125g (5 oz) softened butter**
- ○ **5 eggs**
- ○ **750ml (27 fl oz) milk**
- ○ **250ml (9 fl oz) cream**
- ○ **200g (7 oz) mixed dried fruit**
- ○ **180g (7¼ oz) caster sugar**
- ○ **1ml (¼ tsp) grated nutmeg**
- ○ **2.5ml (½ tsp) powdered cinnamon**

1. Cut the crusts off the bread and trim so as to fit at least 6 slices flat in the bottom of an ovenproof dish. Butter the dish and spread the slices of bread generously with butter on both sides. Arrange the first 6 slices in the dish, sprinkle with half the dried fruit, half the grated nutmeg and half the cinnamon. Arrange another layer of buttered bread on top and the rest of the dried fruit, nutmeg and cinnamon on that. End with a final layer of bread.
2. Bring the milk to the boil in a saucepan. Break the eggs into a bowl, sprinkle in the sugar and whisk until the mixture is smooth. When the milk starts to boil, remove from the heat and stir in the cream. Pour into the egg yolk mixture, whisking continuously; then pour this mixture on to the bread in the cooking dish. Leave to rest for 30 minutes, until the bread has soaked up all the liquid.
3. At the end of that time, set the oven to 200°C (387°F; gas mark 5½). Cover the dish with foil or greaseproof paper and cook for 30 minutes; then continue cooking uncovered for another 30 minutes, until the bread pudding is crisp and golden.
4. Remove from the oven and serve at once in the cooking dish, or leave to cool a little for 10 minutes.

Accompany this pudding with raspberry or apricot jam thinned with a little water.

Gâteau de Poires au Pain Noir

Pear and Brown Bread Pudding

Serves 6. Preparation: 30 min Cooking: 50 min
★

- ○ **200g (7 oz) stale brown bread**
- ○ **125g (5 oz) softened butter**
- ○ **50g (2 oz) almonds**
- ○ **150g (6 oz) soft brown sugar**
- ○ **600g (1 lb 5 oz) pears**
- ○ **1 lemon**
- ○ **5ml (1 tsp) powdered cinnamon**
- ○ **100g (4 oz) currants**
- ○ **30ml (2 tbls) rum**

1. Soak the currants in the rum. Butter a fireproof porcelain soufflé dish 20cm (8 inches) in diameter. Put a large knob of butter on one side and the rest in a bowl.
2. Reserve 30ml (2 tbls) of brown sugar and sprinkle the rest over the butter in the bowl. Cream together well. Stir in the cinnamon and grate in the lemon peel. Mix well. Grate the almonds on the large holes of the grater, then the bread, and add both to the bowl. Mix well and add the currants. Mix once more.
3. Set the oven to 205°C (400°F; gas mark 6). Peel and core the pears, and slice thinly. Arrange one-third of the buttered bread in the dish and place half the pears on top. Put in another layer of the bread and then the rest of the pears. Finish with a layer of bread. Sprinkle the reserved sugar on top and dot with small knobs of the butter. Cook in the oven for 50 minutes.
4. Serve the bread pudding at once, in the cooking dish.

You can use hazelnuts and apples instead of the almonds and pears.

Crêpes Classiques
Traditional Pancakes

20-24 pancakes. Preparation: 10 min (1 hr before cooking)
Cooking: 40 min
★

○ **250g (9 oz) flour**
○ **3 eggs**
○ **½ litre (18 fl oz) milk**
○ **2.5ml (½ tsp) salt**
○ **15ml (1 tbls) caster sugar**
○ **30ml (2 tbls) oil (optional)**

For flavouring:
○ **15ml (1 tbls) rum or 15ml**
   (1 tbls) orange flower water

For cooking:
○ **50g (2 oz) butter**

1. Sift the flour into a bowl. Make a well in the centre and break in the eggs. Add the oil, salt and sugar, with the flavouring and a little milk. Blend all together well, working from the centre out round and round in a circle. Pour the milk in slowly, stirring continuously. When the batter is smooth and well-blended, strain through a sieve into a bowl. Leave to rest for at least one hour.
2. Cook the pancakes. Melt the butter in a frying pan kept only for cooking pancakes; it should be 20cm (8 inches) in diameter. When it has melted, pour off the butter into a bowl; grease the pan with a little of the butter each time before cooking the pancake. When the pan is really hot ladle out a little of the batter into it, and tilt it to spread the batter in an even circle. Cook the pancake on one side and then toss it (or flip it over with a spatula) to cook the other side. The cooking should take about one minute in all.
3. Keep the pancakes warm by piling them on a dish placed over a saucepan filled with boiling water.

Serve with various kinds of jams, or with marron purée, honey, or sugar. You can fill them with slices of apple that have been sugared and sautéed in butter. To make sure of really crisp pancakes, add another egg to the batter and replace half the amount of milk with water. For a lighter pancake, use half milk and half beer; or just water on its own. If the batter is too thick, add a little water just before cooking. Never add more milk – it makes the pancakes heavy.

Crêpes à la Minute
Quick Pancakes

18-24 pancakes. Preparation: 5 min Cooking: 25 min
★

○ **125g (5 oz) flour**
○ **3 eggs**
○ **30ml (2 tbls) oil**
○ **50g (2 oz) melted butter**
○ **1ml (¼ tsp) salt**
○ **15ml (1 tbls) caster sugar**
○ **25g (1 oz) vanilla sugar**
○ **15ml (1 tbls) rum**
○ **350ml (12½ fl oz) milk**
○ **grated peel of ½ orange or**
   lemon (optional)

For cooking:
○ **25g (1 oz) butter approx**

1. For this recipe it is best to use an electric blender or beater. Put the flour, eggs, salt, sugar, vanilla sugar, oil, melted butter, rum, milk and grated peel into a large bowl or in the blender. Beat at the fast speed with the electric beater for 1 minute, then strain the batter through a sieve. This batter does not need to rest because it is so rich in eggs and fats, and so it can be used immediately.
2. Melt the butter in the frying pan. Pour in a little batter, using a small ladle, and tilt the pan all round in a circular movement. After a few seconds of cooking, flip the pancake over with a palette knife or spatula (these pancakes are too thin to be tossed) and cook on the other side for 10 to 12 seconds. In between making each pancake, lightly grease the pan with a cloth or piece of kitchen paper dipped in the melted butter.
3. Stack the pancakes in a pile on a dish placed over a pan of boiling water to keep warm.

Serve the pancakes sprinkled with a little sugar, mixed with vanilla sugar if you like, and with more grated peel. They are also excellent served cold with jam, honey or sugar.

Crêpes Soufflées Citron-Framboises
Lemon Soufflé Pancakes with Raspberry Purée

Serves 6.
Preparation and cooking: 50 min
★ ★

For the batter:
○ **100g (4 oz) flour**
○ **2 eggs**
○ **50g (2 oz) melted butter**
○ **¼ litre (9 fl oz) milk**
○ **15ml (1 tbls) caster sugar**

For the purée:
○ **400g (14 oz) raspberries**
○ **100g (4 oz) icing sugar**
○ **juice of 1 lemon**

For the soufflé:
○ **4 eggs**
○ **2 egg whites**
○ **90ml (6 tbls) caster sugar**
○ **15ml (1 tbls) cornflour**
○ **grated peel of 3 lemons**
○ **15ml (1 tbls) lemon juice**

For cooking:
○ **30g (1¼ oz) butter**

1. Prepare the batter and cook the pancakes following the recipe for a quick pancake batter on page 66. This quantity of batter should give you about 15 pancakes. Put the 12 nicest on one side to fill later with the lemon soufflé. Prepare the raspberry purée: mash the raspberries, using a fork. Stir in the lemon juice and sugar and mix together well until the sugar has dissolved. Keep in the refrigerator. The pancakes and raspberry purée may be prepared a few hours in advance.
2. 25 minutes before serving, prepare the soufflé. Set the oven to 230°C (450°F; gas mark 8). Separate the eggs. Put the yolks in a bowl and sprinkle in half the sugar; beat until the mixture turns pale and frothy. Then stir in the cornflour, lemon juice and grated peel. Beat for another 30 seconds. Whisk the egg whites until stiff, beat in the remaining sugar, and continue beating for another minute. Beat one-quarter of this meringue mixture into the egg yolks, then pour all back on to the rest of the beaten whites and fold in carefully with a spatula.
3. Lightly grease an ovenproof dish. Spread one pancake on a plate and place 2 large tablespoons of the soufflé in the centre. Fold the pancake over and place it in the dish. Repeat with the 11 remaining pancakes, arranging them tightly in the dish. Cook in the oven for 4 minutes, until the pancakes start to open as the soufflé swells up inside them. Bring to the table, and serve the raspberry purée separately.

Crêpes Fourrées Orange-Cassis
Orange Pancakes with Blackcurrant Sauce

Serves 8. Preparation and cooking: 1 hr
★ ★

For the batter:
○ **125g (5 oz) flour**
○ **2 eggs**
○ **1 egg yolk**
○ **¼ litre (9 fl oz) milk**
○ **15ml (1 tbls) caster sugar**
○ **100g (4 oz) melted butter**
○ **grated peel of ½ orange**

For the crème pâtissière:
○ **4 egg yolks**
○ **125g (5 oz) sugar**
○ **60g (2½ oz) flour**
○ **½ litre (18 fl oz) warm milk**
○ **30ml (2 tbls) orange liqueur**
○ **grated peel of 1 orange**

For the sauce:
○ **400g (14 oz) blackcurrants**
○ **100g (4 oz) caster sugar**
○ **30ml (2 tbls) crème de cassis (blackcurrant liqueur)**

1. You may prepare the blackcurrant sauce, pancakes and crème pâtissière a few hours in advance. Purée the blackcurrants to make the sauce, using a mill or blender. Stir in the sugar and the crème de cassis and mix well; chill in the refrigerator.
2. Prepare and cook the pancakes following the recipe for a quick pancake batter on page 66. This quantity of batter should give you about 18 pancakes. You will need 16 so choose the best looking.
3. Prepare the crème pâtissière following the recipe on page 8. Let it cool a little, then stir in the grated orange peel and the liqueur. Mix together well.
4. 10 minutes before serving, set the oven to 220°C (425°F; gas mark 7). Place a large spoonful of the orange-flavoured filling in the centre of each pancake, roll it up like a cigar and arrange in an ovenproof dish. Cook in the oven for 6 minutes.
5. Put 2 pancakes on each plate and pour a little of the blackcurrant sauce around them. Serve immediately.

Make this dessert really special by flaming the pancakes at the moment of serving. Heat 45ml (3 tbls) of orange liqueur and 30ml (2 tbls) of cognac or rum in a small saucepan. Bring hot to the table and set alight. Pour the flaming spirit over the pancakes. It will add a real touch of luxury!

Crêpe Géante aux Cerises

Giant Cherry Pancake

Serves 4. Preparation: 15 min Cooking: 15 min

★

○ **500g (18 oz) cherries**
○ **2 small eggs**
○ **80g (3¼ oz) flour**
○ **150ml (5 fl oz) milk**
○ **60g (2½ oz) butter**
○ **30ml (2 tbls) caster sugar**
○ **1ml (¼ tsp) salt**
○ **30ml (2 tbls) kirsch**

To serve:
○ **30ml (2 tbls) caster sugar**

1. Wash and stone the cherries and put to macerate in a bowl with the sugar and kirsch.
2. Prepare the batter. Melt two-thirds of the butter over a low heat. Sift the flour into a large bowl and make a well in the centre. Add the salt. Separate the eggs and pour the yolks into the well with the melted butter. Mix with a spatula, pouring in the milk a little at a time. When the batter is blended and smooth, add the cherries and their juice. Whisk the egg whites until just stiff and fold into the batter.
3. Over a low heat, melt half the remaining butter in a large frying pan 28cm (11 inches) in diameter. Pour in the batter, spreading the cherries evenly with a spatula. Cover with a lid, and cook over a very low heat for 7 minutes, placing an asbestos sheet in between the pan and heat (if necessary). If the pan does not have a lid, use a plate or round baking tin. When the first side is cooked, turn the pan over so that the pancake falls on to the lid. Add more butter to the frying pan and slide the pancake back to be cooked on the other side for about 7 minutes.
4. When the pancake is golden, and has puffed right up, slide on to a serving dish and sprinkle with sugar. Serve at once.

Crêpe Géante Fourrée aux Pommes

Giant Apple Pancake

Serves 4-6.
Preparation and cooking: 45 min
★

○ **3 apples**
○ **150g (6 oz) flour**
○ **100g (4 oz) caster sugar**
○ **100g (4 oz) melted butter**
○ **3 eggs**
○ **200ml (7 fl oz) milk**
○ **15ml (1 tbls) calvados**
○ **2.5ml (½ tsp) powdered cinnamon**
○ **2.5ml (½ tsp) powdered vanilla**
○ **2.5ml (½ tsp) salt**

1. Sift the flour into a large bowl. Make a well in the centre and break in the eggs; add the salt, half the sugar, vanilla, cinnamon, calvados, and half the melted butter. Mix with a spatula, stirring from the centre outwards in a circular movement. Slowly pour in the milk, stirring continuously. When the batter is smooth and well-blended, strain through a sieve into a measuring jug. You should get about ½ litre (18 fl oz). Leave the batter to rest while you prepare the apples.
2. Slice the apples quite thickly. Put half the remaining butter in a large frying pan 26cm (10½ inches) in diameter and melt over a medium heat. Fry the apple slices on each side for 5 to 7 minutes altogether. Sprinkle with half the remaining sugar halfway through cooking. When they are golden and caramelized, remove and put on one side.
3. Wipe the frying pan and place over a low heat. Put in half the remaining butter and slowly pour in half the batter, spreading it out round the pan from the centre. When it starts to firm arrange the apple slices on it, then slowly pour in the rest of the batter on top. Cover with a lid (if you do not have a large enough lid, use a plate or round baking tin). Cook over a very low heat for 15 minutes.
4. At the end of that time, tilt the pan and slide the pancake out on to the lid. Put the rest of the butter in the frying pan and slide the pancake back to cook on the other side for 15 minutes. Then slide on to a serving dish and serve.

This giant-sized pancake is quite delicious served with sugar and cream, or with calvados.

Crêpes Suzette

Crêpes Suzette

Serves 6. Preparation and cooking: 40 min

★

For the batter:
○ **125g (5 oz) flour**
○ **3 eggs**
○ **30ml (2 tbls) oil**
○ **50g (2 oz) melted butter**
○ **1ml (¼ tsp) salt**
○ **15ml (1 tbls) caster sugar**
○ **25g (1 oz) vanilla sugar**
○ **15ml (1 tbls) rum**
○ **350ml (12½ fl oz) milk**
○ **30g (1¼ oz) butter for cooking**

For the sauce:
○ **100g (4 oz) softened butter**
○ **100g (4 oz) caster sugar**
○ **1 orange or 2 tangerines**
○ **90ml (6 tbls) orange or tangerine liqueur**
○ **45ml (3 tbls) cognac**

1. Prepare and cook 18 thin pancakes or crêpes following the recipe for a quick pancake batter on page 66.
2. 10 minutes before serving, cut the butter into small cubes and put in the frying pan which has been used for cooking the pancakes. Add the sugar, 30ml (2 tbls) of liqueur and 15ml (1 tbls) cognac. Finely grate the peel of the orange or tangerines into the pan. Squeeze the juice and stir in as well. Place over a high heat and boil for 1 minute; you should have a thick syrup. Reduce the heat and leave to simmer over a very low heat.
3. Dip each crêpe, one after the other, in the hot syrup and fold them over twice. Arrange in a large dish placed over a saucepan filled with boiling water to keep them warm. If there is any syrup left, pour it over the crêpes in the dish.
4. Heat the remaining liqueur and cognac in a small saucepan. Bring with the crêpes to the table and light. Pour it, flaming, over the crêpes. When the flame has died out, serve immediately.

No one is agreed whether the classic crêpe Suzette should be flavoured with orange or tangerine. Some prefer one, some the other. Why not try a mixture of both?

Crêpes au Cidre et aux Pommes Rapées

18-20 pancakes. Preparation: 15 min (1 hr before cooking) Cooking: 30 min

Apple Pancakes with Cider

★

○ **250g (9 oz) flour**
○ **4 eggs**
○ **30ml (2 tbls) oil**
○ **300ml (12½ fl oz) milk**
○ **300ml (12½ fl oz) sweet cider**
○ **60ml (4 tbls) caster sugar**
○ **2.5ml (½ tsp) powdered cinnamon**
○ **2.5ml (½ tsp) powdered vanilla**
○ **2.5ml (½ tsp) salt**
○ **500g (18 oz) apples**
○ **40g (1¾ oz) butter**

1. Prepare the batter. Sift the flour into a large bowl, make a well in the centre and break in the eggs. Add the sugar, salt, vanilla, cinnamon and oil. Stir with a spatula, working out from the centre. Pour the milk in slowly, then add the cider, stirring all the time, or mix everything together in an electric blender until smooth. When the batter is well-blended, strain through a fine sieve into a bowl and leave to rest for at least one hour.
2. 5 minutes before cooking the pancakes, peel and core the apples, then grate them, using the large holes of the grater, into the batter. Mix in well.
3. Melt the butter and lightly grease a frying pan 20cm (8 inches) in diameter. Ladle in a little batter and spread it evenly in the pan (using a spatula, if necessary). Cook the pancake slowly on one side, then toss (this should not be difficult because the pancakes are fairly thick) and cook on the other side. Repeat until all the batter is used up. If the batter is too thick, add a little water.

Serve hot, sprinkled with sugar mixed with vanilla, cinnamon and the grated peel of one lemon or orange. You can also flame them with calvados.

Crêpes à l'Unilatérale
One-Sided Pancakes

28 pancakes. Preparation: 15 min Cooking: 20 min

★

- ○ ½ litre (18 fl oz) slightly warm milk
- ○ 4 eggs
- ○ 100g (4 oz) caster sugar
- ○ 100g (4 oz) flour
- ○ 100g (4 oz) melted butter
- ○ 2.5ml (½ tsp) vanilla essence or powdered vanilla
- ○ pinch salt

For cooking:
- ○ 25g (1 oz) butter

1. Separate the eggs. Put the egg whites in a large bowl, together with the salt. Put the yolks in a bowl, sprinkle in the sugar and beat, using a whisk, until the mixture turns pale. Then sprinkle in the flour and continue beating. Add the butter, vanilla, then slowly pour in the milk, still beating all the time.
2. When the batter is smooth and well-blended, whisk the egg whites until just stiff and fold them into the batter, lifting with a spatula. The batter should be light and frothy.
3. Melt the butter in the frying pan, then pour away. Place the pan over a medium heat and pour in some batter, using a ladle – about 30ml (2 tbls). In a few seconds, the bottom of the pancake should be golden and the top covered with tiny holes. As soon as you can slide the spatula underneath it is ready (the top will still be white). Lift up the pancake and roll it towards you, then slide on to a serving dish. Grease the frying pan with a little butter and carry on making the pancakes until there is no batter left. Arrange the pancakes in a dish placed over a saucepan filled with boiling water to keep them warm; or place the dish in a warm oven, once the pancakes are cooked.

This way of cooking pancakes, made with a light and frothy batter, makes them very crisp and smooth. Serve warm, preferably on their own.

Crêpes à la Crème au Parfum de Fleurs
Pancakes with Cream and Flower Water

24 pancakes. Preparation: 10 min (1 hr before cooking) Cooking: 40 min

★

- ○ 250g (9 oz) flour
- ○ 3 eggs
- ○ 3 egg yolks
- ○ ½ litre (18 fl oz) milk
- ○ 150g (6 oz) double cream
- ○ 100g (4 oz) butter
- ○ 2.5ml (½ tsp) salt
- ○ 30ml (2 tbls) sugar

Flavouring:
- ○ 15ml (1 tbls) cognac or maraschino liqueur

To serve:
- ○ 125g (5 oz) soft brown sugar
- ○ orange flower, rose or jasmin water.

1. In a small saucepan, melt 60g (2½ oz) of butter over a low heat. Sift the flour into a large bowl. Make a well and add the salt, sugar, eggs and egg yolks, melted butter, the liqueur to flavour, and a little milk. Work the mixture with a spatula, stirring from the centre out, and slowly pour in the milk. When the batter is blended, stir in the cream. Mix well and strain through a fine sieve into a bowl. Leave to rest for at least one hour.
2. Just before cooking the pancakes, melt the remaining 40g (1¾ oz) butter to grease a frying pan 20cm (8 inches) in diameter. Cook the pancakes and stack them in a pile on a plate placed over a saucepan filled with boiling water to keep warm. Sprinkle each pancake with 5ml (1 tsp) of sugar and a few drops of flower water.
3. Serve the pancakes at once.

Instead of sprinkling the pancakes with soft brown sugar and orange water, you can pour over them an orange-flavoured honey which you have first warmed slightly (you will need to add 5ml (1 tsp) of orange flower water to the batter for extra flavour).

Beignets de Pommes à la Cannelle

Apple Fritters with Cinnamon

Serves 5-6. Preparation: 15 min
(2 hr before cooking) Cooking: 15 min
★

○ **150g (6 oz) flour**
○ **250ml (9 fl oz) beer**
○ **pinch salt**
○ **4 medium-sized apples**
○ **juice of 1 lemon**
○ **60ml (4 tbls) caster sugar**
○ **15ml (1 tbls) powdered cinnamon**
○ **oil for deep frying**

To serve:
○ **icing sugar**

1. Sift the flour into a bowl; make a well in the centre and add the salt. Slowly pour in the beer, working the flour into the liquid with a spatula from the centre out. When the batter is smooth, leave to stand for 2 hours in a warm place.
2. Put the lemon juice together with the same amount of water in a basin. Peel and core the apples, and cut into slices. Dip them in the lemon juice, then sprinkle on both sides with the mixed sugar and cinnamon. Put on one side.
3. Heat the oil in a deep fryer. When it is very hot, but not smoking, wipe the apples and dip each slice in the batter. Then fry in the oil. When golden, turn over and brown on the other side. Remove from the oil with a slotted spoon. Drain on kitchen paper and arrange on a serving dish. Sprinkle with icing sugar and keep in a warm oven while cooking the other fritters.

Beignets de Pommes au Sésame

Apple Fritters with Sesame Seeds

Serves 4. Preparation: 15 min Cooking: 15 min

★★★

○ **2 medium-sized apples**
○ **150g (6 oz) flour**
○ **1 egg**
○ **250g (9 oz) sugar**
○ **15ml (1 tbls) oil**
○ **15ml (1 tbls) toasted sesame seeds**
○ **oil for deep frying**

1. Beat the egg with 150ml (5 fl oz) of water; put the flour in a bowl and slowly pour in the egg and water mixture, stirring with a spatula until the batter is blended.
2. Grease a serving dish with 15ml (1 tbls) of oil. Put 1 litre (1¾ pints) of cold water in a basin together with a dozen ice cubes.
3. Heat the oil in a deep fryer: it should be at least 5cm (2 inches) high. Peel and core the apples, and cut each one into 8, making the pieces roughly square. Add to the batter.
4. Put 15ml (1 tbls) of oil, 100ml (3½ fl oz) of water and the sugar in a frying pan 24cm (9½ inches) in diameter and place over a medium heat until a golden syrup forms.
5. When the oil in the deep fryer is hot but not smoking, remove the apple pieces one by one from the batter with tongs and fry. They should be golden in about one minute. Remove from the oil with a slotted spoon and drain on kitchen paper.
6. Reduce the heat under the caramel as low as possible (place an asbestos sheet between the heat and the frying pan, if necessary), and throw in the sesame seeds, and then the fritters, four at a time. Use a spatula or slice to turn the fritters all over in the caramel; then plunge them in the iced water. Leave in the water for 6 to 8 seconds; remove and place in the serving dish.
7. When all the apple fritters are cooked, bring them immediately to the table. You will enjoy this Chinese delicacy!

Beignets de Bananes au Citron Vert

Banana Fritters with Lime

*Serves 6. Preparation: 15 min
(30 min before cooking) Cooking: 15 min*
★★

- ○ **2 medium-sized bananas**
- ○ **30ml (2 tbls) lime juice**
- ○ **45ml (3 tbls) white rum**
- ○ **45ml (3 tbls) caster sugar**
- ○ **250g (9 oz) flour**
- ○ **1 egg**
- ○ **200ml (7 fl oz) butter**
- ○ **25g (1 oz) butter**
- ○ **2.5ml (½ tsp) baking powder**
- ○ **2 pinches salt**
- ○ **oil for deep frying**

To serve:
- ○ **caster sugar to taste**

1. Peel and cut the bananas across into rounds or lengthways in half. Put in a bowl and moisten with the lime juice and 30ml (2 tbls) of rum; mix together and sprinkle with 30ml (2 tbls) of sugar. Mix once more and leave to stand, turning the banana slices over from time to time.
2. 10 minutes before cooking the fritters, prepare the batter. Melt the butter in a small saucepan over a low heat; then leave to cool. Beat the egg with the milk in a bowl; put the flour in another bowl, stir in the salt, 15ml (1 tbls) of sugar and the baking powder. Then slowly pour in the egg and milk mixture, stirring continuously with a spatula. Add the melted butter and the remaining 15ml (1 tbls) of rum. Mix well until the batter is smooth.
3. Heat the oil in a deep fryer: it should be at least 5cm (2 inches) high. Wipe the banana slices, and dip them in the batter, 6 at a time. When the oil is very hot but not smoking, put in the banana fritters and fry on both sides. Remove from the oil with a slotted spoon and drain on kitchen paper.
4. When the fritters are ready, stack them in a pile and serve at once, sprinkled with sugar, or not – as you wish.

This dessert is a speciality of Martinique.

Beignets d'Ananas au Rhum

Pineapple Fritters with Rum

*Serves 5. Preparation: 15 min (1 hr before cooking)
Cooking: 15 min*
★

- ○ **10 slices of pineapple (tinned in syrup)**
- ○ **150g (6 oz) flour**
- ○ **100ml (3½ fl oz) beer**
- ○ **25g (1 oz) butter**
- ○ **pinch salt**
- ○ **30ml (2 tbls) caster sugar**
- ○ **30ml (2 tbls) white rum**
- ○ **2 egg whites**
- ○ **oil for deep frying**

To serve:
- ○ **icing sugar**

1. One hour before cooking the fritters, drain the pineapple slices well, wipe dry, and put on a plate, moistened with rum and sprinkled with sugar on both sides.
2. Melt the butter in a small saucepan over a low heat. In a bowl, mix the flour, salt, and melted butter. Slowly pour in the beer, together with an equal amount of water, working the flour in with a spatula. When the batter is smooth, leave to stand for one hour.
3. Just before cooking the fritters, heat the oil in a deep fryer: it should be at least 5cm (2 inches) high. Drain the pineapple slices on kitchen paper. Keep the juice. Beat the egg whites until they form soft peaks, and fold in to the batter with the pineapple juice, using a whisk.
4. When the oil is very hot but not smoking, dip the pineapple slices in the batter, then put in the oil. When the fritters are golden on one side, turn over and fry on the other side. Remove from the oil with a slotted spoon and drain on kitchen paper.
5. Arrange the fritters in a serving dish and sprinkle with icing sugar. Eat at once.

Couronne de Pommes

Apple Crown Pudding

Serves 6-8. Preparation 30 min Cooking: 1 hr 30 min
the day before
★

○ **1.5kg (3¼ lb) apples**
○ **500g (18 oz) caster sugar**
○ **1 lemon**
○ **1 vanilla pod**

1. Peel and core the apples, and put the peel and core in a saucepan with ½ litre (18 fl oz) of water. Cut the lemon in half and rub over the quarters of peeled apple, so that they do not discolour. Bring the contents of the saucepan to the boil over a high heat, and cook for 15 minutes, covered, then sieve the contents into another saucepan. This juice, rich in pectin, will set the apples, once cooked.
2. Split the vanilla pod lengthways in half. Put in to the juice, add the sugar as well, and place the saucepan over a high heat. When the syrup has turned nearly golden, throw in the apple quarters, shaking the saucepan to make sure the fruit is coated all over. Reduce the heat. Cook, uncovered, shaking the saucepan from time to time, until the apples become transparent. Do not stir, or else the fruit will disintegrate. It will take from 1 hour to 1 hour 30 minutes to cook them, depending on the quality of the apples.
3. Fill a wetted savarin or ring mould 24cm (9½ inches) in diameter with the cooked apples; remove the vanilla pod, and leave to cool. Then chill in the refrigerator until next day.
4. The next day, turn out on to a serving dish and serve at once.

This apple crown pudding is delicious served with an egg custard sauce, or simply with some double cream.

Pommes en Papillottes

Baked Apples with Redcurrant Jelly

Serves 6. Preparation: 15 min cooking: 45 min
★

○ **6 apples**
○ **30ml (2 tbls) caster sugar**
○ **30ml (2 tbls) redcurrant (or quince) jelly**
○ **6 pinches cinnamon**

1. Set the oven to 220°C (425°F; gas mark 7). Wash and wipe the apples. Cut a small slice off the bottom of each so that they do not roll. Remove the core with a sharp knife, making sure at least 1cm (½ inch) is left at the bottom (if you use an apple corer you are liable to go right through).
2. Put 5ml (1 tsp) of the jelly, with 5ml (1 tsp) of sugar and a pinch of cinnamon inside each apple. Wrap each one up as tightly as possible in foil or greaseproof paper.
3. Arrange the apples in foil on a wire rack in a baking tin and cook in the oven for 45 minutes.
4. When cooked, remove from the oven and bring to the table as they are. Let your guests unwrap their own apples so they can savour the delicious smell themselves!

You may prefer to fill the apples with blossom honey mixed with chopped walnuts and sultanas, instead of the jelly and cinnamon.

If you add a few drops of lemon juice or vinegar to the sugar when making caramel, it will prevent the syrup from crystallizing during cooking – otherwise this will occur whenever you dip a spoon into the caramel or add the nuts – walnuts, hazelnuts, or almonds – to make praline.

Pommes de Pin

Apple Pinecones

Serves 6. Preparation: 20 min Cooking: 30 min

★

○ **6 apples**
○ **60g (2½ oz) butter**
○ **30ml (6 tsp) sultanas**
○ **30ml (6 tsp) caster sugar**
○ **120g (4¾ oz) flaked almonds**

1. Set the oven to 205°C (400°F; gas mark 6). Peel the apples in a spiral, making sure they are as well shaped as possible. Cut a small slice off the bottom of each to stop them from rolling. Remove the core with a sharp knife, leaving at least 1cm (½ inch) at the bottom. (If you use an apple corer you will go right through.)
2. Butter a baking dish large enough to fit all the apples with plenty of room between them. Place them in the dish, and put a little knob of butter inside each, followed in turn by 5ml (1 tsp) of sultanas, 5ml (1 tsp) of sugar, and then another knob of butter. Pour 60ml (4 tbls) of water into the dish.
3. Place in the oven and cook for 30 minutes or more. Check to see if the apples are cooked by piercing with a knife or skewer. It should go in quite easily.
4. While the apples are cooking, put the almonds in a large frying pan over a medium heat. Brown, shaking the pan all the time. Then remove from the heat and put on one side.
5. Remove the apples from the oven and transfer to a serving dish, using a spatula or slice. Spike each apple with the best-looking almonds set closely together so that they look like pinecones. Sprinkle the remaining almonds over, and serve.

Serve these apples lukewarm, if you prefer, accompanied by a crème pâtissière flavoured with rum, or by a sabayon.

Poires-Hérissons

Pear Hedgehogs

Serves 6. Preparation: 15 min Cooking: 20 min

○ **6 large pears**
○ **100g (4 oz) flaked almonds**
○ **24 currants**
○ **1 lemon**
○ **30g (1¼ oz) butter**
○ **30ml (2 tbls) caster sugar**

1. Set the oven to 220°C (425°F; gas mark 7). Cut the lemon in half. Slice the pears lengthways into equal halves. Peel and remove the core, and rub each half with the lemon.
2. Butter a baking dish large enough to hold all the fruit easily. Arrange the pears, flat side down, in it and squeeze the lemon juice over. Sprinkle with sugar. Add 90ml (6 tbls) of water to the dish and cook in the oven for 20 minutes, until the pears are cooked (a knife should pierce them easily). Baste the pears with the cooking juice while they are cooking.
3. Meanwhile, brown the almonds in a frying pan over a medium heat, shaking the pan frequently, to prevent them from burning. Put on one side.
4. Lift the cooked pears carefully on to a serving dish, using a spatula or slice. If any juice is left in the dish, pour it over the pears to glaze them.
5. Spike the pears all over with the almonds, starting from the stalk end: they should look like hedgehogs. Use the currants for eyes. Serve at once, or leave to cool for a while.

Serve with a hot chocolate sauce: 150g (6 oz) chocolate melted with 45ml (3 tbls) of water. Or you can accompany this dessert with an egg custard flavoured with kirsch.

Pommes au Cidre Caramélisées

Serves 6. Preparation and cooking: 45 min

Caramel Apples with Cider   ★

○ **6 large cooking apples**
○ **30ml (2 tbls) currants**
○ **6 shelled walnuts**
○ **50g (2 oz) butter**
○ **200ml (7 fl oz) sweet cider**
○ **150g (6 oz) sugar**
○ **½ lemon**

1. Set the oven to 225°C (412°F; gas mark 7½). Butter a baking dish large enough to hold the apples easily.
2. Peel the apples and rub them with the half lemon. Remove the core using an apple corer and arrange them in the dish.
3. Fill each apple with 5ml (1 tsp) of currants, then one walnut (lightly crushed in your fingers). Divide the remaining butter into 6 and place one knob inside each apple.
4. Pour the cider into the dish and cook in the oven for 30 to 40 minutes, until the apples are tender (when a knife pierces them easily). Baste the apples frequently with their own juice during cooking. At the end of the time, very little juice should be left in the dish.
5. When the apples are cooked, turn the oven off. Prepare the caramel: put the sugar with 45ml (3 tbls) of water in a saucepan and place over a medium heat. Cook until a golden syrup has formed. Pour this syrup over the apples and serve at once.

Pêches Fourrées Flambées

Serves 8. Preparation: 20 min Cooking: 40 min

Flambéed Stuffed Peaches   ★

○ **9 large peaches (not too ripe)**
○ **4 macaroons (preferably Nancy macaroons)**
○ **50g (2 oz) crystallized apricot or lemon**
○ **30g (1¼ oz) butter**
○ **45ml (3 tbls) caster sugar**
○ **250ml (9 fl oz) sweet white or muscat wine**
○ **60ml (4 tbls) maraschino liqueur, kirsch, almond liqueur, or grand marnier**

1. Choose firm, yellow peaches whose stones will come out easily. Set the oven to 200°C (387°F; gas mark 5½). Butter a baking dish large enough to hold 8 peaches.
2. Chop the crystallized fruit finely and crush the macaroons: put both together in a bowl. Peel the smallest and ripest peach and mash up the flesh with a fork. Add to the bowl together with 30ml (2 tbls) of sugar. Mix well.
3. Wash and wipe the remaining peaches and cut right across to remove the stones, but do not separate the two halves. Crack 4 of the stones and take out the kernels. Chop these finely and add to the bowl. Mix well and stuff the peaches with the mixture. Close up and place the whole peaches in the dish, with the slit at the bottom.
4. Pour the wine into the baking dish, sprinkle the peaches with sugar and cook in the oven for 40 minutes, until they feel tender when lightly pressed. Baste frequently with their own juice during cooking.
5. When the peaches are done, remove from oven and lift them carefully on to a serving dish. Pour the juice over. Heat the alcohol of your choosing in a small saucepan and bring hot to the table.
6. Flame the hot alcohol in front of your guests, and pour over the peaches. Serve as soon as the flame has died out.

This dessert may be eaten warm or cold. Serve it with a hot or cold custard (sabayon for example) prepared with the same wine you used to cook the peaches.

Wines: the Finishing Touch

Nowadays excellent quality table wines are within the reach of everyone, though you should expect to pay more for a good vintage wine from one of the famous vineyards, such as Nuits-St-Georges or Schloss Johannisberg Riesling. When buying French wine, look for the *Appellation Contrôlée* label, which is a guarantee of quality.

Below is a guide to the wines that go best with certain foods, but there are no absolute *rules* about which wine to serve with what food – in the end it is your palate that must decide. For a large, formal meal, certain wines traditionally follow each other through the menu and you could serve three or even four wines at one meal. In this case, it is usual to serve dry sherry with the soup, dry white wine with the fish course, claret or burgundy with the meat or game and a white dessert wine or medium sweet champagne with the dessert. For cheese, your guests would return to the claret or burgundy. Certain foods kill the flavour of wine and should therefore be avoided if you are planning to serve wine with the meal. Mint sauce, for example, or any salad with a strong vinaigrette dressing, will destroy the taste of the wine.

Remember that red wines are generally served *chambré*, or at room temperature, to bring out the flavour. Draw the cork at least three or four hours before you plan to drink the wine and let the bottle stand in the kitchen or a warm room. (Never be tempted into putting the bottle in hot water or in front of the fire – the flavour will be ruined.) The exception to the *chambré* rule is Beaujolais, which can be served cool – some people even serve it chilled. White or rosé wines are usually served chilled – the easiest way is to put them in the fridge an hour before serving, or plunge them into an ice bucket, if you have one. Champagne should also be served well chilled and is generally brought to the table in an ice bucket.

Wines to Serve with Food

Oysters, shellfish	Chablis, dry Moselle, Champagne
Fried or grilled fish	Dry Graves, Moselle, Hock, Rosé, Blanc de Blanc
Fish with sauces	Riesling, Pouilly-Fuissé, Chablis
Veal, pork or chicken dishes (served simply)	Rosé, Riesling, a light red wine such as Beaujolais
Chicken or pork served with a rich sauce	Claret, Côte de Rhône, Médoc
Rich meat dishes, steaks, game	Red Burgundy, Rioja, Red Chianti
Lamb or duck	Claret, Beaujolais
Desserts and puddings	White Bordeaux, Sauternes, Entre Deux Mers
Cheese	Burgundy, Rioja, Cabernet Sauvignon

This edition published 1992 by Wordsworth Editions Ltd, 8b East Street, Ware, Hertfordshire.

Copyright © Wordsworth Editions Ltd 1992.

Designed by Tony Selina, The Old Goat Graphic Company, London, England.

ISBN 1-85326-983-2

Printed and bound in Hong Kong by South China Printing Company.